FRY'S INSTANT WORD PUZZLES AND ACTIVITIES

Edward B. Fry, Ph.D.
and
Leslie Anne Perry, Ph.D.

Illustrated by
Carolyn A. Quinton

Prentice-Hall, Inc.
Englewood Cliffs, N.J.

Prentice-Hall International, Inc., *London*
Prentice-Hall of Australia, Pty. Ltd., *Sydney*
Prentice-Hall Canada, Inc., *Toronto*
Prentice-Hall of India Private Ltd., *New Delhi*
Prentice-Hall of Japan, Inc., *Tokyo*
Prentice-Hall of Southeast Asia Pte. Ltd., *Singapore*
Editora Prentice-Hall do Brasil Ltda., *Rio de Janeiro*
Prentice-Hall Hispanoamericana, S.A., *Mexico*

10 9 8 7 6 5 4 3 2 1

Library of Congress Cataloging-in-Publication Data

Fry, Edward Bernard
  Fry's instant word puzzles and activities

  1. Reading games. 2. Reading (Primary) I. Perry,
Leslie Anne. II. Title.
LB1525.55.F79 1987   372.4′14   87-11462

ISBN 0-13-331753-6

Printed in the United States of America

About This Book

The word puzzles and activities in this book are designed to reinforce Fry's Instant Words. Classroom teachers, remedial reading teachers, and special education teachers will all find these materials beneficial for their students. The reproducible puzzles and activity sheets can be used to supplement basal readers or other commercial materials. You may find that some of the pages are also useful in preparing students to take standardized tests.

The section called "How to Use This Book" discusses procedures for introducing The Instant Words to students and for using the various types of activities in this book. You will find it helpful to read through the entire section before using the materials with your students.

The Instant Words

The Instant Words comprise the most important words for reading and writing in the English language. It is absolutely impossible to read or write anything without knowing at least some of these words. The word list is based on research that revealed that 50 percent of all written material (that is, books, magazines, newspapers) is composed of just the first 100 Instant Words. The first 300 Instant Words make up 65 percent of all written material. (For further information on this list, see "The New Instant Word List" by Edward Fry, in the December 1980 issue of *The Reading Teacher.* This list replaces the 1957 version of The Instant Words.)

Students must recognize these words *instantly* for reading fluency and must spell them rapidly and correctly for writing fluency. Students need and learn other subject matter words, like monster or helicopter; The Instant Words are a core vocabulary.

This list is for beginning readers of any age—children or adults. The whole list is usually not mastered for reading until beginning third-grade reading ability is achieved, although some students master it much earlier and others later.

The Instant Words also make an excellent spelling list. If you want more Instant Words, you can find 1,000 of them in *The Reading Teacher's Book of Lists* (Prentice-Hall, 1984) and *The New Reading Teacher's Book of Lists* (Prentice-Hall, 1985).

Teaching Strategies

Teachers should be aware that the supplemental reading and writing activities cover three years of ability range. Don't rush a student through these activities. Take plenty of time for oral and silent story reading, comprehension drills, phonics lessons, and a good variety of activities for teaching students to read.

Be flexible and let some students or groups go through the activities more rapidly than others. Though a strong feature of these activities is their suggested sequence, you are free to omit or repeat selected activities or even to skip students ahead. You are the director of the most important overall activity, "teaching reading."

Edward Fry

Leslie Perry

About the Authors

EDWARD FRY, Ph.D., is a Professor of Education and Director of the Reading Center at Rutgers University in New Brunswick, New Jersey. He is known in the education field for his *Readability Graph, The Instant Words,* and numerous books and articles.

Dr. Fry co-authored *The Reading Teacher's Book of Lists* (Prentice-Hall, 1984) and *The New Reading Teacher's Book of Lists* (Prentice-Hall, 1985), which have become standard classroom teachers' references. He has also done a number of secondary reading drill books for Jamestown Publishers, college textbooks for McGraw-Hill, and videotape adult reading improvement lessons for Time-Life Video.

LESLIE ANNE PERRY, Ph.D., has had a wide range of teaching experiences in reading. She has served as a classroom teacher and a remedial reading specialist at the elementary and junior high school levels and has taught undergraduate and graduate reading education courses.

Dr. Perry is the co-author of *Teaching the Reading Teachers* (Charles C. Thomas, 1983) and *Teaching Basic Skills in Reading* (Charles C. Thomas, 1985).

How to Use This Book

Prior to beginning a unit, you should introduce the words reinforced by that unit. The number of words to be introduced at one time depends on the ability of the students. For students already familiar with some of the words, you may prefer to introduce all ten words at once. On the other hand, some students may not be able to handle more than two or three new words at a time. Regardless of the number of words presented on a given day, all ten words of a unit should be introduced before the students are asked to complete any of the worksheets in that unit.

A number of The Instant Words have multiple meanings. In some cases, both meanings of a word are used. Therefore, you should look over the pages of each new unit to be certain that any multiple meanings are taken into consideration when the words are introduced to the students.

The following procedure can be used for introducing each word:

1. Write the word on the chalkboard.
2. Point to the word and pronounce it clearly and distinctly. Then have the students repeat the word several times as you point to it. Finally, call on various students to say the word.
3. Say the word again and then spell it, pointing to each letter as you say its name. Then have the students say the word and spell it as you point to each letter.
4. Use the word orally in a sentence or phrase. Then write on the chalkboard a sentence or phrase containing the word. Finally, read what you wrote, then have the students read it with you.

After a group of words has been introduced, the students should be given the opportunity to practice recognizing the words. The words can be written on flashcards and prominently displayed. Spare moments throughout the school day (before lunch, after lunch, etc.) can then be used to check individual students on their ability to recognize the words. Reading specialists and other teachers who work with a number of different groups of students each day can integrate practice on these words with other activities during class sessions.

When you are ready to begin a unit, you have the option of beginning it with either the "Flashcards" page or the "Write the Words" page. Suggestions for using both of these types of pages appear later.

Word Boxes

All the pages in each unit contain word boxes. These boxes feature either all ten of the words reinforced in that unit, or half (five) of the words from the unit. Before the students begin work on *each and every worksheet,* you should have them say the words in the word box. The words can also be written on the chalkboard and you can call on various students to read them. *This repetition is needed in order for the students to retain the words!*

Additional Nouns

Additional nouns (nouns not included in the 300 Instant Words) have been added to many of the pages. Each of these nouns is accompanied by a picture at the top of the page. You should go over these words with the students before having them complete the page. The students should be informed that these words will appear in the sentences they are going to read. Therefore, if they come to a word in a sentence that they do not know, a good strategy is to look at the pictures and their labels to see if the unknown word is identified there.

Eighty additional nouns have been added to The Instant Words on various activity pages throughout the book. They appear in their noun groups in the following units:

Unit 15	Unit 16	Unit 17	Unit 18
School Workers	Clothing	Writing Tools	Zoo Animals
teacher	shirt	pen	elephant
bus driver	pants	pencil	giraffe
secretary	dress	crayon	bear
principal	shoes	typewriter	tiger
custodian	hat	computer	monkey

Unit 19	Unit 20	Unit 21	Unit 22
Toys	School Items	Growing Things	Outdoor Things
ball	marker	bush	sun
doll	scissors	flower	moon
train	paste	grass	star
game	ruler	corn	cloud
skateboard	chalkboard	tomatoes	rain

Unit 23	Unit 24	Unit 25	Unit 26
Pets	Workers	Farm Animals	Transportation
cat	farmer	horse	bicycle
dog	police officer	cow	truck
rabbit	cook	pig	bus
bird	doctor	chicken	plane
fish	nurse	duck	boat

Unit 27	Unit 28	Unit 29	Unit 30
Furniture	Entertainment	Eating Objects	Buildings
table	television	cup	store
chair	radio	plate	gas station
sofa	movie	bowl	church
chest	ballgame	fork	theater
desk	band	spoon	barn

Additional Verbs

Additional verbs (verbs not included in The Instant Words) listed below have been added to twelve of the units. The twelve extra verbs are accompanied by drawings. These drawings illustrate the action that is named by the verb. The first of these additional verbs appears in Unit 6. As with the additional nouns, the students' attention needs to be directed to the pictures at the top of the page as these extra verbs are used in the sentences that the students will read. The additional verbs are:

Unit 6	Unit 9	Unit 12	Unit 15
climb	drink	fly	draw
Unit 18	Unit 21	Unit 23	Unit 26
jump	wash	sleep	ride
Unit 27	Unit 28	Unit 29	Unit 30
sit	listen	laugh	sing

Fry's Instant Word Criterion Test

This test can be used to assess a child's knowledge of the 300 Instant Words. The test is useful for keeping a record of a child's knowledge and for reporting.

Progress Chart

Included in this book is a Progress Chart that can be used to keep track of the progress of each student. Students often find it motivating to keep a record of their own progress. The chart also gives you a handy record that can be kept in a file folder.

Answer Keys

Answer keys are provided at the end of the book to facilitate checking. You may want to have your students check some of the pages in class to provide additional practice in reading the words.

DIRECTIONS FOR USING THE "FLASHCARDS"

The flashcards for each unit can be cut out and retained by the students for use in a variety of activities. Suggested activities include:

1. *Peer Tutoring.* One child can hold up a word for the other children in a small group (or a single child) to read. This activity can be made more interesting if the tutor flashes the card by turning it over quickly or briefly exposing it from behind a book. Students who miss words can later be given more practice. Also, flashcards from several units can be combined. For more durability, duplicate or photocopy the flashcards on heavy paper.

2. *Tachistoscope.* Flashcard pages can be reproduced on heavy paper and cut up the middle. The word strips can then be used in teacher-made (or student-made) tachistoscopes.

3. *Know and Don't Know Piles.* An individual student can sort through a group of flashcards placing the known words in a Know Pile and the unknown words in a Don't Know Pile. Later a tutor can check to see if the Know words are indeed known and can help the student with the words in the Don't Know Pile.

4. *Board Games.* Flashcards can also be used with either commercial or teacher-made (sometimes student-made) board games. The boards can have a theme of race cars, horses, boats, and so forth. Typically a board features a track with spaces. A student throws dice or spins a spinner and moves a marker the indicated number of spaces if the word on the flashcard pile is correctly read. If the student does not read the word correctly, the turn is lost.

5. *Word Endings.* Word endings can be added to many of the flashcards to create new words. These endings can be added to some of the words in Units 1–10: s, ing, ed. These endings are commonly used with some of the words in Units 11–30: s, ing, ed, er, ly, est.

You may choose to use the flashcards as an introduction to each unit. They may, however, be used at any time. The flashcards also provide an excellent review of words taught in earlier lessons so students should be instructed to save the cards.

DIRECTIONS FOR USING
THE "WRITE THE WORDS" PAGES

The purpose of these pages is to provide students with practice in recognizing the letter sequence of the words in each unit. While writing a word, a student's attention is automatically directed toward the letters and their sequence.

Before the students write the words in their proper spaces, they can write them with their fingers in the air. After completing the page, the students can take out a blank sheet of paper and write the words a second time using this procedure: (1) study a word on the "Write the Words" page, (2) write the word (from memory) on the second sheet of paper, and (3) check the newly written word by referring back to the original page.

It is recommended that students use manuscript (printing) rather than cursive when they complete the "Write the Words" pages. This procedure allows for greater attention to the individual letters in the words. Also, when students later meet these words in other contexts, the words will be printed rather than written in cursive.

DIRECTIONS FOR USING
THE "FIND THE WORDS" PAGES

To complete these pages, the students search for the hidden words in the puzzles and circle them. The Level B "Find the Words" puzzles are more difficult than the Level A puzzles. The words in the Level A puzzles all appear horizontally, whereas, in the Level B puzzles, words appear horizontally (left to right only), vertically (top to bottom only), or diagonally (left to right only, but slanting either up or down).

Some students may be confused by little words that are part of bigger words (for example, *he—the*) or by a word that inadvertently appears in a puzzle but is not one of the words introduced in that unit. Therefore, you should instruct your students to look for and circle only the ten Instant Words that are reinforced in the unit in which the puzzle appears.

DIRECTIONS FOR USING THE "MATCH SENTENCES WITH PICTURES" PAGES (UNITS 1–10)

On these pages, the students are required to read each sentence and draw a line to the picture that best illustrates what the sentence is about.

Before the students begin work on a page, you should read the directions to them. As mentioned earlier, you should also have them say the words in the word box.

After the students complete the page, they should reread the sentences to make certain that they chose the proper picture for each sentence. In the early units, it is possible for students to respond correctly to some of the items by reading only the noun in the sentence. Therefore, you may wish to assess your students' recognition of The Instant Words in the unit by having them read the sentences orally when they have completed the page.

DIRECTIONS FOR USING THE "MATCH PICTURES WITH SENTENCES" PAGES (UNITS 11–20)

To complete these pages, the students will read both sentences beside each picture and will then choose the sentence that better describes or tells about what is shown in the picture. They will draw a line from the picture to the sentence they select.

After you read the directions and have the students say the words in the word box and the words under the pictures, you should then stress the importance of reading both sentences in their entirety before selecting the one that goes with the picture. In many cases, there exists only a slight difference between the two sentences. Therefore, careful reading is necessary.

When the students have completed their work, they should read over the sentences a final time to check the accuracy of their choices. You may wish to have the students check their papers by calling on various students to read the sentences they have chosen.

DIRECTIONS FOR USING THE "WRITE THE WORDS IN SENTENCES" PAGES (UNITS 21–30)

These pages provide students with practice in writing the words in sentences. Students are to read each sentence and select a word from the word box to complete the sentence. After they write the word in the space, they should then reread the sentence in its entirety to make certain that they have selected a word that *makes sense* in the context of the sentence.

Some students may get confused and select words that appear under the pictures on some of the pages. They should be cautioned to select only the words that appear in the word box.

DIRECTIONS FOR USING THE "CHOOSE THE CORRECT WORDS" PAGES

The format used on these pages differs slightly among each set of ten units. In Units 1–10, the students are to complete the sentences by selecting from two words printed directly above the writing spaces. For Units 11–20, the two word choices appear at the end of the sentences. Units 21–30 have three word choices at the end of each sentence.

Regardless of the format, the students will perform essentially the same task on all of the pages of this type. They will (1) read a sentence and select the best word to complete that sentence, (2) write the selected word in the space, and (3) reread the sentence to check the accuracy of their choice.

DIRECTIONS FOR USING THE "JUST FOR FUN" PAGES

A "Just for Fun" page is included at the end of each unit. These pages provide additional practice with the words presented in that unit. Five types of "Just for Fun" pages are included; suggestions for their use follow.

Word Scramble

On the Word Scramble pages, the words from the unit have been scrambled. The students are to put the letters of each word back in their proper order by correctly writing the word on the line beside its scrambled form. To simplify the procedure, they can cross off each word in the word box as they use it.

Pages of this type can be difficult for young children or children of limited ability. If your students have difficulty with these pages, the pages can be completed as a group activity, or they can be omitted.

Missing Letters

The words on the Missing Letters pages all have one letter missing. The students will fill in the missing letters to spell the words from the word box. They will then copy the entire word on the line below its corresponding picture.

As an extension of this activity, some students may enjoy creating a Missing Letters page for their classmates to complete.

Anagrams

The Anagrams pages contain the letters needed to spell the words from the unit where the page appears. The students should cut out the letters and spread them out on their desks.

To avoid confusion, letters that might be reversed by the students (for example, u and n) have lines printed under them. Students should be told that when the line is at the bottom, the letter is *right side up*.

After the students have cut out the letters, they can arrange them to spell the

Instant Words reinforced by that unit. They can either spell each word as you pronounce it or they can spell the words independently by selecting them from the word box. If students are to spell each word by looking at it in the word box, they should be instructed to use care when cutting out the letters and not to throw away the portion of the page containing the word box.

Word Mazes

To complete the word mazes, the students should be instructed to trace over each maze to spell a word from the word box. They can trace over the path first with their fingers and then with a pencil, mentally spelling the word as they pass over each letter. After the students have traced over a maze/word, they should then write the word on the line below the maze.

After completing the page, some students may wish to draw word mazes of their own on a separate sheet of paper.

Letter Squares

On these pages, each word from the word box is missing one or more letters. The students will spell the words by writing the missing letters in the squares. After they have completed a word, they should copy it on the line below the squares.

Your students may find this activity is easier if they cross off the words in the word box as they use them.

DIRECTIONS FOR CONTINUED REINFORCEMENT/REVIEW

As was noted earlier, the flashcards can be retained by the students and used to review words from previous units. Also, the Know—Don't Know activity described earlier can be expanded into a word bank activity where students keep their cards in a small box or *word bank*. The students should be periodically checked on the words in their *banks* to make certain that they have not forgotten previously learned words. Words they don't know can be retaught.

Additional reinforcement can be provided by using the words from previous units in spelling, handwriting, and creative-writing lessons. Students are more likely to remember words if they are given frequent opportunities to use them.

If, after completing a number of units, you discover that many of the students do not seem to know previously taught words, some reteaching may be necessary. As these units build on each other, with each new unit containing words from previous units, students can become lost if they did not adequately learn the words from those earlier units. It is a fact of life that some students require more (sometimes many more!) exposures to words than other students in order to master those words. For these students, it may be necessary to repeat entire units. As with other materials, the goal should be to help the students learn the words, not simply to cover the material.

Fry's Instant Word Criterion Test

The test on the following pages can save you a lot of time by testing a child's knowledge of the 300 Instant Words. Teach only what the child doesn't know.

To find out which words the child knows, have him or her read from one copy of the test while you check each known word on your copy of the test.

In order to save even more time, use the Quick Survey Test first. This test is the first three words of each column. Ask the child to read all the words in the Quick Survey Test for a page (not the whole 100 words on the page). If the child knows all the words in the Quick Survey you can assume that he or she knows most of the words on that page, so you can now go on to the next page.

If the child makes two or more mistakes, you had better test the whole page. As you can see from looking at the test, there are ten words in each unit. If the child makes a mistake in any unit, then you can use the drills in this book to teach the words in that unit.

This Instant Words criterion test is useful for keeping a record of a child's knowledge and for reporting. You might want to keep a copy of the test in each child's folder so that you can test-teach-test-teach, and so forth. In other words, you can test until you find a weakness, teach by having the child do the unit, then test again to find the next weakness.

Fry's Instant Word Criterion Test also makes an excellent record of progress. You might want to administer it at the beginning of the year and again at the end of the year, or after a shorter period, to show progress. A record of accomplishment will help you at report-card time and in parent conferences.

This is a "criterion test," which means that it measures a child's knowledge against a criterion—in this case, the criterion is the 300 Instant Words. The other more formal type of test is called a standardized or normed test. These tests compare a child's knowledge with a norm or standardization group. They yield scores like Grade Equivalent scores and Percentile scores. But the criterion test tells you how well a child is progressing toward a criterion, in other words, how much of the subject matter the child knows. Criterion tests such as this one also suggest what should be taught next.

Fry's Instant Word Criterion Test will work well with beginning readers of any age: young children, remedial reading or special education students (both elementary and secondary) or even illiterate adults. It will also help you to individualize instruction in your class; each student or small group can be working on a different unit of the drills.

FRY'S INSTANT WORDS CRITERION TEST—First Hundred

Quick Survey Test of Words in Units 1–10

Unit 1

1. ☐ the
2. ☐ of
3. ☐ and
4. ☐ a
5. ☐ to

6. ☐ in
7. ☐ is
8. ☐ you
9. ☐ that
10. ☐ it

Unit 2

11. ☐ he
12. ☐ was
13. ☐ for
14. ☐ on
15. ☐ are

16. ☐ as
17. ☐ with
18. ☐ his
19. ☐ they
20. ☐ I

Unit 3

21. ☐ at
22. ☐ be
23. ☐ this
24. ☐ have
25. ☐ from

26. ☐ or
27. ☐ one
28. ☐ had
29. ☐ by
30. ☐ word

Unit 4

31. ☐ but
32. ☐ not
33. ☐ what
34. ☐ all
35. ☐ were

36. ☐ we
37. ☐ when
38. ☐ your
39. ☐ can
40. ☐ said

Unit 5

41. ☐ there
42. ☐ use
43. ☐ an
44. ☐ each
45. ☐ which

46. ☐ she
47. ☐ do
48. ☐ how
49. ☐ their
50. ☐ if

Unit 6

51. ☐ will
52. ☐ up
53. ☐ other
54. ☐ about
55. ☐ out

56. ☐ many
57. ☐ then
58. ☐ them
59. ☐ these
60. ☐ so

Unit 7

61. ☐ some
62. ☐ her
63. ☐ would
64. ☐ make
65. ☐ like

66. ☐ him
67. ☐ into
68. ☐ time
69. ☐ has
70. ☐ look

Unit 8

71. ☐ two
72. ☐ more
73. ☐ write
74. ☐ go
75. ☐ see

Unit 9

76. ☐ number
77. ☐ no
78. ☐ way
79. ☐ could
80. ☐ people

81. ☐ my
82. ☐ than
83. ☐ first
84. ☐ water
85. ☐ been

86. ☐ call
87. ☐ who
88. ☐ oil
89. ☐ now
90. ☐ find

Unit 10

91. ☐ long
92. ☐ down
93. ☐ day
94. ☐ did
95. ☐ get

96. ☐ come
97. ☐ made
98. ☐ may
99. ☐ part
100. ☐ over

FRY'S INSTANT WORDS CRITERION TEST—Second Hundred

Quick Survey Test of Words in Units 11–20

Unit 11
101. ☐ new
102. ☐ sound
103. ☐ take

126. ☐ great
127. ☐ where
128. ☐ help

Unit 16
151. ☐ put
152. ☐ end
153. ☐ does

176. ☐ kind
177. ☐ hand
178. ☐ picture

104. ☐ only
105. ☐ little

129. ☐ through
130. ☐ much

154. ☐ another
155. ☐ well

179. ☐ again
180. ☐ change

Unit 12
Unit 14
Unit 17
Unit 19

106. ☐ work
107. ☐ know
108. ☐ place
109. ☐ year
110. ☐ live

131. ☐ before
132. ☐ line
133. ☐ right
134. ☐ too
135. ☐ mean

156. ☐ large
157. ☐ must
158. ☐ big
159. ☐ even
160. ☐ such

181. ☐ off
182. ☐ play
183. ☐ spell
184. ☐ air
185. ☐ away

Unit 12
111. ☐ me
112. ☐ back
113. ☐ give
114. ☐ most
115. ☐ very

136. ☐ old
137. ☐ any
138. ☐ same
139. ☐ tell
140. ☐ boy

Unit 17
161. ☐ because
162. ☐ turn
163. ☐ here
164. ☐ why
165. ☐ ask

186. ☐ animal
187. ☐ house
188. ☐ point
189. ☐ page
190. ☐ letter

Unit 15
Unit 20

116. ☐ after
117. ☐ thing
118. ☐ our
119. ☐ just
120. ☐ name

141. ☐ follow
142. ☐ came
143. ☐ want
144. ☐ show
145. ☐ also

166. ☐ went
167. ☐ men
168. ☐ read
169. ☐ need
170. ☐ land

191. ☐ mother
192. ☐ answer
193. ☐ found
194. ☐ study
195. ☐ still

Unit 13
Unit 18

121. ☐ good
122. ☐ sentence
123. ☐ man
124. ☐ think
125. ☐ say

146. ☐ around
147. ☐ form
148. ☐ three
149. ☐ small
150. ☐ set

171. ☐ different
172. ☐ home
173. ☐ us
174. ☐ move
175. ☐ try

196. ☐ learn
197. ☐ should
198. ☐ America
199. ☐ world
200. ☐ high

© 1987 by Prentice-Hall, Inc. From Fry's Instant Word Puzzles and Activities, E. Fry and L. Perry

FRY'S INSTANT WORDS CRITERION TEST—Third Hundred

Quick Survey Test of Words in Units 21–30

Unit 21

201. ☐ every
202. ☐ near
203. ☐ add

Unit 26

251. ☐ until
252. ☐ children
253. ☐ side

276. ☐ idea
277. ☐ enough
278. ☐ eat

---

204. ☐ food
205. ☐ between

229. ☐ while
230. ☐ along

254. ☐ feet
255. ☐ car

279. ☐ face
280. ☐ watch

Unit 24

206. ☐ own
207. ☐ below
208. ☐ country
209. ☐ plant
210. ☐ last

231. ☐ might
232. ☐ close
233. ☐ something
234. ☐ seem
235. ☐ next

256. ☐ mile
257. ☐ night
258. ☐ walk
259. ☐ white
260. ☐ sea

Unit 29

281. ☐ far
282. ☐ Indian
283. ☐ real
284. ☐ almost
285. ☐ let

Unit 22

211. ☐ school
212. ☐ father
213. ☐ keep
214. ☐ tree
215. ☐ never

236. ☐ hard
237. ☐ open
238. ☐ example
239. ☐ begin
240. ☐ life

Unit 27

261. ☐ began
262. ☐ grow
263. ☐ took
264. ☐ river
265. ☐ four

286. ☐ above
287. ☐ girl
288. ☐ sometimes
289. ☐ mountain
290. ☐ cut

Unit 25

216. ☐ start
217. ☐ city
218. ☐ earth
219. ☐ eye
220. ☐ light

241. ☐ always
242. ☐ those
243. ☐ both
244. ☐ paper
245. ☐ together

266. ☐ carry
267. ☐ state
268. ☐ once
269. ☐ book
270. ☐ hear

Unit 30

291. ☐ young
292. ☐ talk
293. ☐ soon
294. ☐ list
295. ☐ song

Unit 23

221. ☐ thought
222. ☐ head
223. ☐ under
224. ☐ story
225. ☐ saw

246. ☐ got
247. ☐ group
248. ☐ often
249. ☐ run
250. ☐ important

Unit 28

271. ☐ stop
272. ☐ without
273. ☐ second
274. ☐ late
275. ☐ miss

296. ☐ leave
297. ☐ family
298. ☐ body
299. ☐ music
300. ☐ color

Name _____ **Date** _____

PROGRESS CHART

Color in or mark box for each unit completed. You could enter the date in each box as the units are completed.

FIRST HUNDRED INSTANT WORDS

Unit 1	Unit 2	Unit 3	Unit 4	Unit 5	Unit 6	Unit 7	Unit 8	Unit 9	Unit 10

SECOND HUNDRED INSTANT WORDS

Unit 11	Unit 12	Unit 13	Unit 14	Unit 15	Unit 16	Unit 17	Unit 18	Unit 19	Unit 20

THIRD HUNDRED INSTANT WORDS

Unit 21	Unit 22	Unit 23	Unit 24	Unit 25	Unit 26	Unit 27	Unit 28	Unit 29	Unit 30

Table of Contents

Unit 1: the, of, and, a, to, in, is, you, that, it

Flashcards

Write the Words

Find the Words—Level A

Match Sentences with Pictures—I

Match Sentences with Pictures—II

Find the Words—Level B

Choose the Correct Words

Just-for-Fun Word Scramble

Unit 2: he, was, for, on, are, as, with, his, they, I

Flashcards

Write the Words

Find the Words—Level A

Match Sentences with Pictures—I

Match Sentences with Pictures—II

Find the Words—Level B

Choose the Correct Words

Just-for-Fun Missing Letters

Unit 3: at, be, this, have, from, or, one, had, by, word

Flashcards

Write the Words

Find the Words—Level A

Match Sentences with Pictures—I

Match Sentences with Pictures—II

Find the Words—Level B

Choose the Correct Words

Just-for-Fun Anagrams

Unit 16: put, end, does, another, well, large, must, big, even, such

Flashcards
Write the Words
Find the Words—Level A
Match Pictures with Sentences—I
Match Pictures with Sentences—II
Find the Words—Level B
Choose the Correct Words
Just-for-Fun Word Scramble

Unit 17: because, turn, here, why, ask, went, men, read, need, land

Flashcards
Write the Words
Find the Words—Level A
Match Pictures with Sentences—I
Match Pictures with Sentences—II
Find the Words—Level B
Choose the Correct Words
Just-for-Fun Missing Letters

Unit 18: different, home, us, move, try, kind, hand, picture, again, change

Flashcards
Write the Words
Find the Words—Level A
Match Pictures with Sentences—I
Match Pictures with Sentences—II
Find the Words—Level B
Choose the Correct Words
Just-for-Fun Anagrams

Unit 19: off, play, spell, air, away, animal, house, point, page, letter

Flashcards
Write the Words
Find the Words—Level A
Match Pictures with Sentences—I
Match Pictures with Sentences—II
Find the Words—Level B
Choose the Correct Words
Just-for-Fun Word Mazes

Unit 24: might, close, something, seem, next, hard, open, example, begin, life

Flashcards
Write the Words
Find the Words—Level A
Write the Words in Sentences—I
Write the Words in Sentences—II
Find the Words—Level B
Choose the Correct Words
Just-for-Fun Word Mazes

Unit 25: always, those, both, paper, together, got, group, often, run, important

Flashcards
Write the Words
Find the Words—Level A
Write the Words in Sentences—I
Write the Words in Sentences—II
Find the Words—Level B
Choose the Correct Words
Just-for-Fun Letter Squares

Unit 26: until, children, side, feet, car, mile, night, walk, white, sea

Flashcards
Write the Words
Find the Words—Level A
Write the Words in Sentences—I
Write the Words in Sentences—II
Find the Words—Level B
Choose the Correct Words
Just-for-Fun Word Scramble

Unit 27: began, grow, took, river, four, carry, state, once, book, hear

Flashcards
Write the Words
Find the Words—Level A
Write the Words in Sentences—I
Write the Words in Sentences—II
Find the Words—Level B
Choose the Correct Words
Just-for-Fun Missing Letters

Name _____   Date _____

Unit 1: FLASHCARDS

Directions: Cut out the flashcards and use them to help you learn the words.

the, of, and, a, to, in, is, you, that, it

the	in
of	is
and	you
a	that
to	it

Unit 1: WRITE THE WORDS

Directions: Write the words in the spaces.

| the, of, and, a, to, in, is, you, that, it |

the

the

1. _____

of

2. _____

and

3. _____

a

4. _____

to

5. _____

in

6. _____

is

7. _____

you

8. _____

that

9. _____

it

10. _____

Unit 1: FIND THE WORDS—LEVEL A

Directions: There are 10 Instant Words hidden here.
Can you find and circle them?
Here are the words to look for:

a, in, it, that, to, and, is, of, the, you

```
N  F  H  Y  I  J  A
Z  N  I  T  B  L  Q
I  N  D  J  T  H  E
O  F  T  Y  O  U  H
T  H  A  T  A  N  D
X  R  S  T  O  I  S
B  C  S  O  K  L  Z
```

Unit 1: MATCH SENTENCES WITH PICTURES—I

Directions: Draw a line from each sentence to the picture it tells about.

| the, a, in, is, that |

dog   cat   fish   bird   hat   car

1. The cat is in the car.

a.

2. That is a bird.

b.

3. A fish is in the hat.

c.

4. That is a dog.

d.

5. A cat is in that hat.

e.

6. That fish is in the car!

f.

Name _____ Date _____

Unit 1: MATCH SENTENCES WITH PICTURES—II

Directions: Draw a line from each sentence to the picture it tells about.

of, and, to, you, it

bird   cat   dog   fish   rabbit   picture

1. That is a picture of a cat.   a.

2. It is to you.   b.

3. That is a picture of a dog and a rabbit.   c.

4. It is to the dog.   d.

5. It is a fish and a bird.   e.

6. Is that you?   f.

Unit 1: FIND THE WORDS—LEVEL B

Directions: There are 10 Instant Words hidden here.
Can you find and circle them?
Here are the words to look for:

| a, in, it, that, to, and, is, of, the, you |

```
O  B  U  X  J  J  X  U
F  N  D  M  M  T  O  O
T  N  X  N  F  Y  H  J
A  L  K  J  E  L  I  E
T  I  L  S  B  T  S  L
V  H  T  K  J  Q  O  G
I  M  A  L  N  L  D  O
L  E  Q  T  C  A  N  O
```

© 1987 by Prentice-Hall, Inc. Fry's Instant Word Puzzles and Activities. E. Fry and L. Perry

Name _____ **Date** _____

Unit 1: CHOOSE THE CORRECT WORDS

Directions: Choose the correct word to complete each sentence and write the word in the space.

the, of, and, a, to, in, is, you, that, it

bird   cat   dog   fish   hat   picture

that   of

1. A bird is in _____ hat.

a   and

2. It is a dog _____ a cat.

is   the

3. The cat is in _____ hat.

of   to

4. That is a picture _____ a fish.

and   you

5. It is to _____ .

in   it

6. A bird is _____ the picture.

Unit 1: JUST-FOR-FUN WORD SCRAMBLE

Directions: Unscramble the mixed-up words below. Write the correct word from the word box on each line.

> the, of, and, a, to, in, is, you, that, it

1. si ＿＿＿＿＿＿＿＿＿＿＿

2. atth ＿＿＿＿＿＿＿＿＿

3. eht ＿＿＿＿＿＿＿＿＿

4. ti ＿＿＿＿＿＿＿＿＿＿

5. a ＿＿＿＿＿＿＿＿＿＿

6. fo ＿＿＿＿＿＿＿＿＿＿

7. adn ＿＿＿＿＿＿＿＿＿

8. ni ＿＿＿＿＿＿＿＿＿＿

9. uyo ＿＿＿＿＿＿＿＿＿

10. ot ＿＿＿＿＿＿＿＿＿

© 1987 by Prentice-Hall, Inc. *Fry's Instant Word Puzzles and Activities,* E. Fry and L. Perry.

Name _____ **Date** _____

Unit 2: FLASHCARDS

Directions: Cut out the flashcards and use them to help you learn the words.

he, was, for, on, are, as, with, his, they, I

he	as
was	with
for	his
on	they
are	I

Name _____   **Date** _____

Unit 2: WRITE THE WORDS

Directions: Write the words in the spaces.

| he, was, for, on, are, as, with, his, they, I |

he

1. __he__ _____   as

    6. _____

was

2. _____   with

    7. _____

for

3. _____   his

    8. _____

on

4. _____   they

    9. _____

are

5. _____   I

    10. _____

Name _____   Date _____

Unit 2: FIND THE WORDS—LEVEL A

Directions: There are 10 Instant Words hidden here.
Can you find and circle them?
Here are the words to look for:

> are, for, his, on, was, as, he, I, they, with

```
T  H  E  Y  Q  U  H
F  O  R  W  A  S  R
O  Q  A  R  E  K  I
C  E  H  E  H  F  F
L  R  D  W  I  T  H
C  R  B  Y  P  A  S
H  I  S  O  N  D  M
```

Unit 2: MATCH SENTENCES WITH PICTURES—I

Directions: Draw a line from each sentence to the picture it tells about.

| he, for, are, with, they |

boy   girl   cat   car

1. The car is for the boy.   a.

2. He is with the girl.   b.

3. They are in the car.   c.

4. He is with the cat.   d.

5. They are with the cat.   e.

6. That cat is for the girl.   f.

Unit 2: MATCH SENTENCES WITH PICTURES—II

Directions: Draw a line from each sentence to the picture it tells about.

| was, on, as, his, I |

  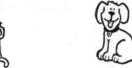 

girl   cat   dog   car

1. The girl was in the car.   a.

2. The car is his.   b.

3. The cat and I are on a car.   c.

4. It is his dog.   d.

5. He and I are on that car.   e.

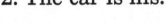

6. As the dog was in the car...   f.

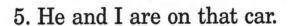

Unit 2: FIND THE WORDS—LEVEL B

Directions: There are 10 Instant Words hidden here.
Can you find and circle them?
Here are the words to look for:

| are, for, his, on, was, as, he, I, they, with |

```
D  D  N  W  R  P  Q  U
T  Q  F  O  A  A  H  V
H  H  F  Z  A  S  E  N
O  I  E  P  R  B  O  K
J  W  S  Y  E  G  M  H
D  C  X  F  S  N  T  K
X  Q  W  E  B  I  M  L
M  W  K  V  W  H  V  I
```

Name _____ **Date** _____

Unit 2: CHOOSE THE CORRECT WORDS

Directions: Choose the correct word to complete each sentence and write the word in the space.

he, was, for, on, are, as, with, his, they, I

cat   chair

1.   was   with

   He _____ on the chair.

2.   as   are

   They _____ on a chair.

3.   for   his

   He is with _____ cat.

4.   They   I

   _____ are with his cat.

5.   he   on

   It is _____ that chair.

6.    as   for

   It is _____ you.

Name _____   **Date** _____

Unit 2: JUST-FOR-FUN MISSING LETTERS

Directions: The words on the fish are each missing a letter. Fill in the missing
letters to spell the words from the word box. Then copy the completed
words on the lines below the fish.

> he, was, for, on, are, as, with, his, they, I

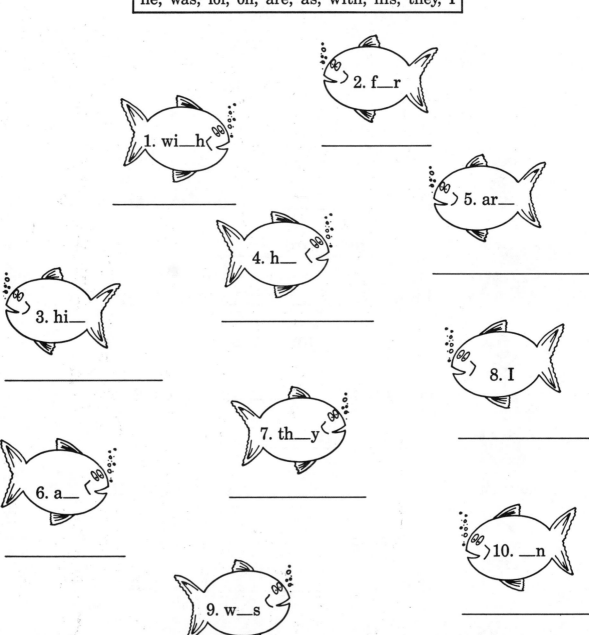

1. wi__h

2. f__r

3. hi__

4. h__

5. ar__

6. a__

7. th__y

8. I

9. w__s

10. __n

© 1987 by Prentice-Hall, Inc. *Fry's Instant Word Puzzles and Activities,* E. Fry and L. Perry

Name _____ **Date** _____

Unit 3: FLASHCARDS

Directions: Cut out the flashcards and use them to help you learn the words.

at, be, this, have, from, or, one, had, by, word

at	or
be	one
this	had
have	by
from	word

Unit 3: WRITE THE WORDS

Directions: Write the words in the spaces.

> at, be, this, have, from, or, one, had, by, word

at

1. at

be

2. _____

this

3. _____

have

4. _____

from

5. _____

or

6. _____

one

7. _____

had

8. _____

by

9. _____

word

10. _____

© 1987 by Prentice-Hall, Inc. Fry's Instant Word Puzzles and Activities, E. Fry and L. Perry

Unit 3: FIND THE WORDS—LEVEL A

Directions: There are 10 Instant Words hidden here.
Can you find and circle them?
Here are the words to look for:

> be, from, have, or, word, at, by, had, one, this

```
J E O N E B E
A T H I S E M
W S P X B Z L
O G V H K O R
O K Z F R O M
H A V E H A D
B Y W O R D Z
```

Unit 3: MATCH SENTENCES WITH PICTURES—I

Directions: Draw a line from each sentence to the picture it tells about.

at, this, have, one, had

 cow   duck horse   pig  barn

1. His horse is at this barn.   a.

2. He had a pig.   b.

3. This duck is at the barn.   c.

4. He had a duck.   d.

5. They have one horse and one cow.   e.

6. They have one pig.   f.

Name _____ Date _____

Unit 3: MATCH SENTENCES WITH PICTURES—II

Directions: Draw a line from each sentence to the picture it tells about.

be, from, or, by, word

boy   cow   horse   barn

1. That cow is by the barn.   a.

2. Is that for his cow or his horse?   b.

3. You have to be in the barn!   c.

4. Is this from you?   d.

5. The boy is by the barn.   e.

6. Is this the word *horse* or the word *cow*?   f.

Unit 3: FIND THE WORDS—LEVEL B

Directions: There are 10 Instant Words hidden here.
Can you find and circle them?
Here are the words to look for:

> at, by, had, one, this, be, from, have, or, word

```
N  Z  K  N  M  G  N  L
B  K  F  R  O  M  O  I
E  Y  U  E  A  V  N  E
B  W  K  A  B  U  E  L
O  H  O  A  T  H  I  S
J  R  A  R  J  L  C  D
X  L  S  V  D  Q  A  Z
V  Y  I  X  E  H  S  B
```

Name _____ Date _____

Unit 3: CHOOSE THE CORRECT WORDS

Directions: Choose the correct word to complete each sentence and write the word in the space.

at, be, this, have, from, or, one, had, by, word

man   cow   horse   pig   barn

<u>have   be</u>

1. I have to _____ this pig.

<u>or   from</u>

2. The man had a horse _____ his barn.

<u>by   be</u>

3. I have to _____ at the barn.

<u>or   one</u>

4. Is this cow for you _____ for the man?

<u>by   be</u>

5. One pig is _____ the cow.

<u>had   one</u>

6. This is _____ word for you.

Unit 3: JUST-FOR-FUN ANAGRAMS

Directions: Cut apart the letters on this page. Use the letters to spell each of the words in the word box.

| at, be, this, have, from, or, one, had, by, word |

a	b	d	e
f	h	i	m
n	o	r	s
t	v	w	y

Name _____   Date _____

Unit 4: FLASHCARDS

Directions: Cut out the flashcards and use them to help you learn the words.

but, not, what, all, were, we, when, your, can, said

but	**we**
not	**when**
what	**your**
all	**can**
were	**said**

Unit 4: WRITE THE WORDS

Directions: Write the words in the spaces.

| but, not, what, all, were, we, when, your, can, said |

but

1. but

we

6. _____

not

2. _____

when

7. _____

what

3. _____

your

8. _____

all

4. _____

can

9. _____

were

5. _____

said

10. _____

Unit 4: FIND THE WORDS—LEVEL A

Directions: There are 10 Instant Words hidden here.
Can you find and circle them?
Here are the words to look for:

all, can, said, were, when, but, not, we, what, your

```
W  E  S  K  C  A  N  M
X  R  U  X  V  B  C  Q
E  A  W  H  A  T  W  D
N  O  T  W  E  R  E  T
Z  Y  O  U  R  Z  O  Z
S  A  I  D  W  H  E  N
S  N  O  J  H  L  J  L
A  L  L  I  O  B  U  T
```

Name _____ **Date** _____

Unit 4: MATCH SENTENCES WITH PICTURES—I

Directions: Draw a line from each sentence to the picture it tells about.

not, all, when, can, said

girl

man

cow

duck

horse

1. This duck can have all of it.   a.

2. The girl said, "When can I be on the   b.
   horse?"

3. The cow is not with the man.   c.

4. You can all be by the duck.   d.

5. The man said, "You can have this cow."   e.

6. He said, "When can I have a horse?"   f.

Name _____ Date _____

Unit 4: MATCH SENTENCES WITH PICTURES—II

Directions: Draw a line from each sentence to the picture it tells about.

| but, what, were, we, your |

boy   cow   horse   barn

1. We were with your cow.   a.

2. "Is that your horse?" said the boy.   b.

3. The boy is by the barn but the horse is not.   c.

4. "What can I have?" said the boy.   d.

5. We were at the barn but the cow was not.   e.

6. What is in it?   f.

Unit 4: FIND THE WORDS—LEVEL B

Directions: There are 10 Instant Words hidden here.
Can you find and circle them?
Here are the words to look for:

> all, can, said, were, when, but, not, we, what, your

```
Q  L  K  N  O  R  L  F  H
Q  A  L  B  U  W  G  G  W
I  L  I  W  Y  W  H  E  N
Y  L  L  T  E  H  Z  U  W
O  S  C  W  S  A  I  D  K
U  B  W  A  Q  T  E  L  S
R  A  U  E  N  O  T  M  R
D  V  V  T  R  C  V  Y  S
F  S  E  T  S  E  C  E  T
```

© 1987 by Prentice-Hall, Inc. *Fry's Instant Word Puzzles and Activities,* E. Fry and L. Perry.

Name _____   **Date** _____

Unit 4: CHOOSE THE CORRECT WORDS

Directions: Choose the correct word to complete each sentence and write the word in the space.

> but, not, what, all, were, we, when, your, can, said

boy   duck   pig

__your   said__

1.   Is this _____ word?

__were   all__

2.   You can not have _____ that.

__were   but__

3.   The duck is in it _____ the pig is not.

__We   What__

4.   _____ were all in it.

__your   were__

5.   "When we _____ all in it, the duck was not," said the boy.

__When   What__

6.   _____ is that?

Unit 4: JUST-FOR-FUN WORD MAZES

Directions: Start at the arrow and trace over each maze to spell a word from the word box. Then copy the words on the lines below the mazes.

but, not, what, all, were, we, when, your, can, said

1.

_____

2.

_____

3.

_____

4.

_____

5.

_____

6.

_____

7.

_____

9.

_____

8.

_____

10.

_____

© 1997 by Prentice Hall, Inc. Instant Word Puzzles and Activities, E. Fry and J. Perry

Name _____   Date _____

Unit 5: FLASHCARDS

Directions: Cut out the flashcards and use them to help you learn the words.

there, use, an, each, which, she, do, how, their, if

there	**she**
use	**do**
an	**how**
each	**their**
which	**if**

Unit 5: WRITE THE WORDS

Directions: Write the words in the spaces.

there, use, an, each, which, she, do, how, their, if

there

1. there

use

2. _____

an

3. _____

each

4. _____

which

5. _____

she

6. _____

do

7. _____

how

8. _____

their

9. _____

if

10. _____

Unit 5: FIND THE WORDS—LEVEL A

Directions: There are 10 Instant Words hidden here.
Can you find and circle them?
Here are the words to look for:

> do, how, she, there, which, an, each, if, their, use

```
L  T  H  E  R  E  W  X
R  C  J  H  O  W  U  I
L  X  P  W  H  I  C  H
G  E  Q  U  S  E  W  W
S  H  E  K  H  M  A  O
U  F  C  F  V  A  A  N
T  H  E  I  R  I  F  V
D  O  L  E  A  C  H  I
```

Name _____ **Date** _____

Unit 5: MATCH SENTENCES WITH PICTURES—I

Directions: Draw a line from each sentence to the picture it tells about.

use, an, each, which, she

boy   girl   elephant   fork   spoon   pencil

1. She can use a pencil.

a.

2. Which fork is for you?

b.

3. Which fork can an elephant use?

c.

4. Each girl can use a spoon.

d.

5. An elephant can not use a spoon.

e.

6. Each boy can have a pencil.

f.

Name _____ **Date** _____

Unit 5: MATCH SENTENCES WITH PICTURES—II

Directions: Draw a line from each sentence to the picture it tells about.

 | there, do, how, their, if |

elephant   giraffe   monkey   chair   pencil

1. There is an elephant with a monkey.   a.

2. How do you do that?   b.

3. What do you do if you have an
   elephant in your chair?   c.

4. There is their monkey.   d.

5. Do you have a pencil that I can have?   e.

6. Is that their giraffe?   f.

Unit 5: FIND THE WORDS—LEVEL B

Directions: There are 10 Instant Words hidden here.
Can you find and circle them?
Here are the words to look for:

| an, each, if, their, use, do, how, she, there, which |

```
A  H  O  W  C  F  U  Q  E
D  X  C  T  A  W  Q  V  A
O  G  V  F  H  S  V  P  C
M  B  W  K  I  E  I  F  H
T  H  E  R  E  H  I  J  P
U  S  E  N  C  I  U  R  X
Z  J  A  I  S  H  E  A  B
J  H  H  E  Y  E  O  H  S
G  W  C  F  V  Z  B  E  W
```

Name _____ Date _____

Unit 5: CHOOSE THE CORRECT WORDS

Directions: Choose the correct word to complete each sentence and write the word in the space.

there, use, an, each, which, she, do, how, their, if

 boy   girl  elephant   pencil

there   their
_____

1.  The boy and girl are with _____ elephant.

Which   How
_____

2. _____ pencil can you use?

If   She
_____

3. _____ can use that pencil.

If   Each
_____

4.  _____ girl is by an elephant.

do   each
_____

5. An elephant can not _____ that.

There   How
_____

6. _____ can he be there?

Unit 5: JUST-FOR-FUN LETTER SQUARES

Directions: Write the missing letters in the squares to spell the words from the word box. Then copy the completed words on the lines below the squares.

| there, use, an, each, which, she, do, how, their, if |

1. | t | h | | i | |

   _____

2. | s | | |

   _____

3. | | n |

   _____

4. | | | i | c | h |

   _____

5. | t | h | | r | |

   _____

6. | e | | | |

   _____

7. | | s | |

   _____

8. | d | |

   _____

9. | | f |

   _____

10. | h | | |

   _____

Unit 6: FLASHCARDS

Directions: Cut out the flashcards and use them to help you learn the words.

will, up, other, about, out, many, then, them, these, so

will	many
up	then
other	them
about	these
out	so

Unit 6: WRITE THE WORDS

Directions: Write the words in the spaces.

will, up, other, about, out, many, then, them, these, so

will

will

1. _____

up

2. _____

other

3. _____

about

4. _____

out

5. _____

many

6. _____

then

7. _____

them

8. _____

these

9. _____

so

10. _____

Name _____ **Date** _____

Unit 6: FIND THE WORDS—LEVEL A

Directions: There are 10 Instant Words hidden here.
Can you find and circle them?
Here are the words to look for:

> about, other, so, then, up, many, out, them, these, will

```
U  P  Y  R  M  R  S  O
E  J  C  A  T  H  E  M
H  N  P  Y  J  L  U  O
P  O  T  H  E  R  C  N
L  E  A  B  O  U  T  E
U  D  J  T  H  E  S  E
M  A  N  Y  T  H  E  N
W  I  L  L  O  U  T  N
```

Name _____ ~~te~~ _____

Unit 6: MATCH SENTENCES WITH PICTURES—I

Directions: Draw a line from each sentence to the picture it tells about.

will, up, about, out, these

climb   boy   chicken   bear   mountain   tree

1. The bear is up in the tree.　　a.

2. The bear is out of the tree.　　b.

3. The boy is about to climb up the tree.　　c.

4. These can not climb up the tree.　　d.

5. Will the boy climb out of the tree?　　e.

6. The bear will climb up the mountain.　　f.

Name _____

Unit 6: MATCH SENTENCES WITH PICTURES—II

Directions: Draw a line from each sentence to the picture it tells about.

other, many, then, them, so

climb   girl   chicken   mountain   tree

1. Which tree will the other girl climb?   a.

2. So many of them are on the mountain.   b.

3. So many of them are in the tree.   c.

4. Then he will climb out of the tree.   d.

5. Then the other girl will climb up the mountain.   e.

6. That chicken is for them.   f.

Unit 6: FIND THE WORDS—LEVEL B

Directions: There are 10 Instant Words hidden here.
Can you find and circle them?
Here are the words to look for:

about, other, so, then, up, many, out, them, these, will

```
Q  J  N  L  Y  S  D  C  A
M  K  T  N  I  A  D  Z  F
A  B  A  H  R  V  X  N  G
B  M  R  M  E  T  O  S  X
O  T  E  K  R  S  H  U  I
U  H  J  J  L  G  E  E  C
T  U  O  O  W  I  L  L  N
R  S  P  T  F  X  S  K  I
O  T  H  E  R  U  T  C  Y
```

Unit 6: CHOOSE THE CORRECT WORDS

Directions: Choose the correct word to complete each sentence and write the word in the space.

| will, up, other, about, out, many, then, them, these, so |

climb   girl   bear   book   mountain   tree

other about

1.   This book is _____ a bear.

These Then

2.   _____ will not climb out of the tree.

then them

3.   The bear is by _____ .

Many These

4. _____ of them were up in that tree.

_So Up_

5. _____ she will climb up the mountain with the other girl.

about other

6.  Will the _____ bear climb up in the tree?

Name _____   **Date** _____

Unit 6: JUST-FOR-FUN WORD SCRAMBLE

Directions: Unscramble the mixed-up words below. Write the correct word from the word box on each line.

> will, up, other, about, out, many, then, them, these, so

1. aymn _____

2. os _____

3. rhoet _____

4. liwl _____

5. uto _____

6. ehmt _____

7. taubo _____

8. neht _____

9. pu _____

10. eshte _____

Name _____ **Date** _____

Unit 7: FLASHCARDS

Directions: Cut out the flashcards and use them to help you learn the words.

some, her, would, make, like, him, into, time, has, look

some	him
her	into
would	time
make	has
like	look

Name _____ **Date** _____

Unit 7: WRITE THE WORDS

Directions: Write the words in the spaces.

> some, her, would, make, like, him, into, time, has, look

some

1. some _____

her

2. _____

would

3. _____

make

4. _____

like

5. _____

him

6. _____

into

7. _____

time

8. _____

has

9. _____

look

10. _____

Name _____ Date _____

Unit 7: FIND THE WORDS—LEVEL A

Directions: There are 10 Instant Words hidden here.
Can you find and circle them?
Here are the words to look for:

has, him, like, make, time, her, into, look, some, would

```
T  I  M  E  G  H  I  X
G  R  Q  G  D  G  R  L
L  I  K  E  S  O  M  E
H  A  S  U  H  E  R  T
W  L  B  W  O  U  L  D
I  M  A  K  E  L  R  V
Q  H  I  M  I  N  T  O
L  O  O  K  F  N  A  P
```

Name _____ Date _____

Unit 7: MATCH SENTENCES WITH PICTURES—I

Directions: Draw a line from each sentence to the picture it tells about.

> her, like, him, time, look

 rabbit   tiger   book   picture

1. The rabbit was with him.   a.

2. He will like to look at the book about   b.
   a rabbit.

3. The book is for her.   c.

4. What time can you be there?   d.

5. What will she look like?   e.

6. Look at the picture of the tiger.   f.

Name _____ **Date** _____

Unit 7: MATCH SENTENCES WITH PICTURES—II

Directions: Draw a line from each sentence to the picture it tells about.

some, would, make, into, has

fish

rabbit

tiger

picture

1. Some of them are by the rabbit.   a.

2. She has a rabbit with her.   b.

3. She has some fish.   c.

4. The tiger was into the fish.   d.

5. Would you like to have this tiger?   e.

6. She will make a picture for him.   f.

Name _____ **Date** _____

Unit 7: FIND THE WORDS—LEVEL B

Directions: There are 10 Instant Words hidden here.
Can you find and circle them?
Here are the words to look for:

has, him, like, make, time, her, into, look, some, would

```
R  L  U  T  K  W  L  B  I
L  R  V  O  H  A  S  Q  F
N  A  O  P  B  T  H  E  R
W  L  V  A  W  X  I  D  X
F  O  G  F  M  W  Y  M  E
Z  Q  U  I  L  E  S  M  E
K  G  H  L  K  I  O  F  H
E  W  E  A  D  S  K  S  X
Q  F  M  I  N  T  O  E  H
```

Name _____ Date _____

Unit 7: CHOOSE THE CORRECT WORDS

Directions: Choose the correct word to complete each sentence and write the word in the space.

some, her, would, make, like, him, into, time, has, look

fish   rabbit   tiger   book   picture

<u>like   look</u>

1.    He has time to _____ at the other book.

<u>into   some</u>

2.    She will make a picture of _____ fish.

<u>Would   Make</u>

3.   _____ you like to have this rabbit?

<u>her   him</u>

4.   The picture is of _____ .

<u>has   time</u>

5.   She _____ a picture of a tiger on her book.

<u>time   into</u>

6.    We have _____ to make one other picture.

Unit 7: JUST-FOR-FUN MISSING LETTERS

Directions: The words on the popcorn bags are each missing a letter. Fill in the missing letters to spell the words from the word box. Then copy the completed words on the lines below the popcorn bags.

some, her, would, make, like, him, into, time, has, look

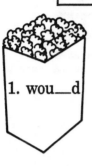

1. wou__d

2. lik__

3. lo__k

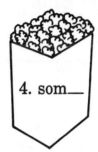

4. som__

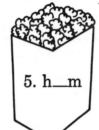

5. h__m

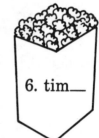

6. tim__

7. h__r

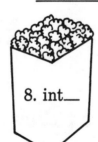

8. int__

9. mak__

10. ha__

© 1987 by Prentice-Hall, Inc. *Fry's Instant Word Puzzles and Activities*, E. Fry and L. Perry.

Name _____ Date _____

Unit 8: FLASHCARDS

Directions: Cut out the flashcards and use them to help you learn the words.

two, more, write, go, see, number, no, way, could, people

two	number
more	no
write	way
go	could
see	people

Name _____ **Date** _____

Unit 8: WRITE THE WORDS

Directions: Write the words in the spaces.

two, more, write, go, see, number, no, way, could, people

two

two

1. _____

more

2. _____

write

3. _____

go

4. _____

see

5. _____

number

6. _____

no

7. _____

way

8. _____

could

9. _____

people

10. _____

Unit 8: FIND THE WORDS—LEVEL A

Directions: There are 10 Instant Words hidden here.
Can you find and circle them?
Here are the words to look for:

could, more, number, see, way, go, no, people, two, write

```
T W O J O W A Y F
H N U M B E R A Q
H P E O P L E G O
K K O F L L C V R
N O F C W S T E L
N U R J D S E E U
C W I N N X L R G
Y K X W R I T E D
M O R E C O U L D
```

Name _____ **Date** _____

Unit 8: MATCH SENTENCES WITH PICTURES—I

Directions: Draw a line from each sentence to the picture it tells about.

| write, go, see, number, people |

man   children   plane   school   book

1. The children will each write a book at school.   a.

2. The man will write a book about people.   b.

3. Many people can go on this plane.   c.

4. See the number on that.   d.

5. These children can go see the plane.   e.

6. A number of people were at the school.   f.

Unit 8: MATCH SENTENCES WITH PICTURES—II

Directions: Draw a line from each sentence to the picture it tells about.

two, more, no, way, could

men   children   plane   picture

1. Which way do I go to the plane?   a.

2. Could you make a picture for them?   b.

3. Two more men will be on the plane.   c.

4. She has no time to look for it.   d.

5. He has two children with him.   e.

6. He will look some more for it.   f.

Unit 8: FIND THE WORDS—LEVEL B

Directions: There are 10 Instant Words hidden here.
Can you find and circle them?
Here are the words to look for:

> could, more, number, see, way, go, no, people, two, write

```
R  S  B  C  S  O  K  L  Z  Y
O  Y  N  D  O  S  E  W  R  W
C  E  Y  U  N  C  M  W  N  U
E  A  E  H  M  W  O  O  B  O
W  G  O  U  C  B  R  U  R  P
P  E  O  P  L  E  E  I  L  E
R  T  I  I  V  N  X  R  T  D
K  N  V  S  Y  Q  S  W  X  E
A  Z  Q  E  B  U  X  J  J  X
N  M  M  E  T  W  O  O  T  X
```

Unit 8: CHOOSE THE CORRECT WORDS

Directions: Choose the correct word to complete each sentence and write the word in the space.

| two, more, write, go, see, number, no, way, could, people |

  man  children   plane   book

number   write

1.  The two children will _____ a book.

more   could

2.  Two _____ people were at the plane.

way   more

3.  There is no _____ he can go on that.

could   number

4.  A _____ of people were on the plane.

no   go

5.  The children will _____ see a man write a book.

see   way

6.  We will go _____ the plane when it is not up.

Unit 8: JUST-FOR-FUN ANAGRAMS

Directions: Cut apart the letters on this page. Use the letters to spell each of the
words in the word box.

two, more, write, go, see, number, no, way, could, people

a	b	c	d	e
e	g	i	l	m
n	o	p	r	s
t	u	w	y	☺

Name _____ Date _____

Unit 9: FLASHCARDS

Directions: Cut out the flashcards and use them to help you learn the words.

my, than, first, water, been, call, who, oil, now, find

my	call
than	who
first	oil
water	now
been	find

Unit 9: WRITE THE WORDS

Directions: Write the words in the spaces.

> my, than, first, water, been, call, who, oil, now, find

my

<big>my</big>

1. _____

than

2. _____

first

3. _____

water

4. _____

been

5. _____

call

6. _____

who

7. _____

oil

8. _____

now

9. _____

find

10. _____

Unit 9: FIND THE WORDS—LEVEL A

Directions: There are 10 Instant Words hidden here.
Can you find and circle them?
Here are the words to look for:

> been, find, my, oil, water, call, first, now, than, who

```
Z  J  B  E  E  N  O  W
C  F  I  R  S  T  E  W
F  S  F  I  N  D  M  Y
T  W  A  T  E  R  F  V
U  E  T  H  A  N  P  G
W  H  O  C  A  L  L  Y
D  O  I  L  M  L  L  U
X  M  V  S  Z  Y  K  Z
```

Name _____ **Date** _____

Unit 9: MATCH SENTENCES WITH PICTURES—I

Directions: Draw a line from each sentence to the picture it tells about.

first, water, call, oil, find

drink   boy   girl

1. She will call to find out where he is.   a.

2. That girl can drink water from it.   b.

3. See the oil go up.   c.

4. The boy will be first to drink the water.   d.

5. We can find oil if we look.   e.

6. He will be the first to call the number.   f.

Name _____ **Date** _____

Unit 9: MATCH SENTENCES WITH PICTURES—II

Directions: Draw a line from each sentence to the picture it tells about.

my, than, been, who, now

drink   boy   dog   school

1. Who has been into the oil?   a.

2. There were more people than I could see.   b.

3. My dog was with them.   c.

4. Now who can that be?   d.

5. I have been at school all this time.   e.

6. The boy will drink his water now.   f.

Unit 9: FIND THE WORDS—LEVEL B

Directions: There are 10 Instant Words hidden here.
Can you find and circle them?
Here are the words to look for:

been, find, my, oil, water, call, first, now, than, who

```
B  I  O  Q  T  L  O  Q  G
W  E  F  A  D  X  T  F  M
F  A  E  N  G  F  H  I  Q
T  M  T  N  Z  T  A  N  Z
M  Y  D  E  S  D  N  D  O
O  I  L  R  R  N  P  H  Q
U  Q  I  F  V  N  W  Z  D
P  F  B  K  J  W  O  G  M
D  C  X  C  A  L  L  W  F
```

Name _____ Date _____

Unit 9: CHOOSE THE CORRECT WORDS

Directions: Choose the correct word to complete each sentence and write the word in the space.

my, than, first, water, been, call, who, oil, now, find

drink   dog

_____ first   find _____

1.  Who will be the _____ to call?

_____ Been   My _____

2. _____ dog can drink that water.

_____ oil   than _____

3. They will look for _____ .

_____ now   been _____

4. His dog has _____ in the water!

_____ now   find _____

5.  She can not _____ him now.

_____ Who   Than _____

6.  _____ will call you?

Unit 9: JUST-FOR-FUN WORD MAZES

Directions: Start at the arrow and trace over each maze to spell a word from the word box. Then copy the words on the lines below the mazes.

| my, than, first, water, been, call, who, oil, now, find |

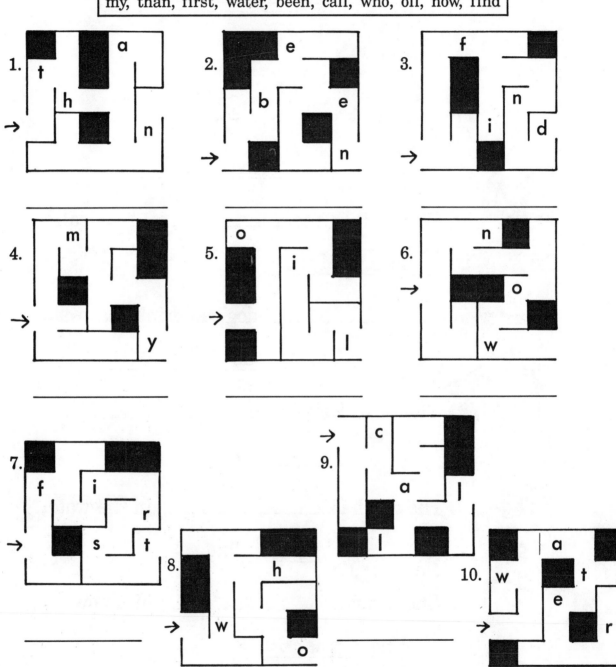

Name _____   **Date** _____

Unit 10: FLASHCARDS

Directions: Cut out the flashcards and use them to help you learn the words.

long, down, day, did, get, come, made, may, part, over

long	come
down	made
day	may
did	part
get	over

Unit 10: WRITE THE WORDS

Directions: Write the words in the spaces.

long, down, day, did, get, come, made, may, part, over

long

1. __long__

down

2. _____

day

3. _____

did

4. _____

get

5. _____

come

6. _____

made

7. _____

may

8. _____

part

9. _____

over

10. _____

Name _____   Date _____

Unit 10: FIND THE WORDS—LEVEL A

Directions: There are 10 Instant Words hidden here.
Can you find and circle them?
Here are the words to look for:

come, did, long, may, own, day, get, made, over, part

```
W  S  E  L  O  N  G
O  V  E  R  O  W  N
F  D  A  Y  D  I  D
M  A  Y  J  A  I  F
X  C  O  M  E  N  C
G  E  T  P  A  R  T
W  B  M  A  D  E  D
```

Name _____   **Date** _____

Unit 10: MATCH SENTENCES WITH PICTURES—I

Directions: Draw a line from each sentence to the picture it tells about.

long, down, day, part, over

eye　　face　　feet　　hand　　head　　sun

1. He has long feet.

a.

2. She has her hand over her head.

b.

3. What day is it?

c.

4. He has his hand down on his feet.

d.

5. Your eye is part of your face.

e.

6. The sun was over them all day long.

f.

Name _____ Date _____

Unit 10: MATCH SENTENCES WITH PICTURES—II

Directions: Draw a line from each sentence to the picture it tells about.

did, get, come, made, may

dog

book

picture

1. May we come in?

a.

2. She made a picture of her dog.

b.

3. He made a book about a dog.

c.

4. How did you get your dog to come with you?

d.

5. Did you get that picture for me?

e.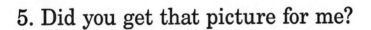

6. May I look at your book?

f.

Unit 10: FIND THE WORDS—LEVEL B

Directions: There are 10 Instant Words hidden here.
Can you find and circle them?
Here are the words to look for:

come, did, long, may, own, day, get, made, over, part

```
R  W  I  T  C  O  X  V
U  X  R  R  O  B  W  T
P  A  E  R  M  O  G  N
P  U  E  T  E  M  Z  O
G  V  E  L  P  W  A  E
O  G  K  O  D  I  D  Y
K  J  U  N  T  A  A  G
S  L  S  G  M  D  K  S
```

Name _____   **Date** _____

Unit 10: CHOOSE THE CORRECT WORDS

Directions: Choose the correct word to complete each sentence and write the word
in the space.

| long, down, day, did, get, come, made, may, part, over |

picture

dog

<u>   day   did   </u>

1.   What _____ you get from them?

<u>   long   part   </u>

2.   He made a picture of a _____ dog.

<u>   over   may   </u>

3.   Can you come _____ some day?

<u>   made   down   </u>

4.   Come _____ from there!

<u>   get   part   </u>

5.   What day did you _____ that from
him?

<u>   may   over   </u>

6.   His dog can go _____ that.

Unit 10: JUST-FOR-FUN LETTER SQUARES

Directions: Write the missing letters in the squares to spell the words from the word box. Then copy the completed words on the lines below the squares.

long, down, day, did, get, come, made, may, part, over

1. □ i □

_____

2. m □ □ e

_____

3. □ □ □ g

_____

4. d □ □ n

_____

5. d a □

_____

6. m a □

_____

7. o □ □ □

_____

8. □ e □

_____

9. p □ □ □

_____

10. c □ □ □

_____

Name _____   Date _____

Unit 11: FLASHCARDS

Directions: Cut out the flashcards and use them to help you learn the words.

new, sound, take, only, little, work, know, place, year, live

new	work
sound	know
take	place
only	year
little	live

Name _____ **Date** _____

Unit 11: WRITE THE WORDS

Directions: Write the words in the spaces.

new, sound, take, only, little, work, know, place, year, live

new   work

1. _____   6. _____

sound   know

2. _____   7. _____

take   place

3. _____   8. _____

only   year

4. _____   9. _____

little   live

5. _____   10. _____

Name _____   Date _____

Unit 11: FIND THE WORDS—LEVEL A

Directions: There are 10 Instant Words hidden here.
Can you find and circle them?
Here are the words to look for:

| know, live, only, sound, work, little, new, place, take, year |

```
O  N  L  Y  I  T  A  K  E
N  E  W  L  I  V  E  P  I
Y  Q  U  P  K  N  O  W  W
D  I  P  E  N  F  D  C  D
U  S  O  U  N  D  A  S  N
N  P  L  A  C  E  H  S  I
W  O  R  K  Y  E  A  R  T
H  L  V  W  L  G  J  C  S
W  H  L  I  T  T  L  E  X
```

Unit 11: MATCH PICTURES WITH SENTENCES—I

Directions: Draw a line from each picture to the sentence that tells about it.

| little, work, know, place, year |

 rabbit   desk   school

1.
a. School is the place I work.
b. School is the place other people get oil.

2.
a. She will go in this little place.
b. She will go to school this year.

3.
a. I made my desk at school.
b. I work at my desk at school.

4.
a. I know what year it is.
b. I know how to do my work.

5.
a. I do a little work each day.
b. I will write a word on the school.

6.
a. The little rabbit will do his work at school.
b. The little rabbit will come to him.

Name _____ Date _____

Unit 11: MATCH PICTURES WITH SENTENCES—II

Directions: Draw a line from each picture to the sentence that tells about it.

| new, sound, take, only, live |

boy   rabbit   school

1.
     a. This work is new to the boy.
     b. The boy is in her way.

2.
     a. My rabbit and I can live in this.
     b. My rabbit can live in this.

3.
     a. I can only find one rabbit.
     b. Take your time when you do your work.

4.
     a. He will not make a sound when he is at work.
     b. He will live at the school all year.

5.
     a. The people made a new sound.
     b. She will only take two.

6.
     a. Which one is for the rabbit?
     b. These are all new.

Name _____ **Date** _____

Unit 11: FIND THE WORDS—LEVEL B

Directions:　There are 10 Instant Words hidden here.
Can you find and circle them?
Here are the words to look for:

know, live, only, sound, work, little, new, place, take, year

```
G  N  D  I  W  F  N  W  X  K
S  E  Z  X  H  D  H  L  R  G
T  W  G  V  H  M  E  O  P  M
A  P  O  N  L  Y  W  N  I  Y
K  P  L  I  T  T  L  E  W
E  L  S  A  W  Y  X  I  O  B
Y  D  O  U  C  F  E  N  H  T
E  Q  U  Z  V  E  K  A  G  M
S  C  N  L  I  V  E  I  R  I
F  D  D  F  H  A  Y  Q  E  U
```

Name _____ Date _____

Unit 11: CHOOSE THE CORRECT WORDS

Directions: Choose the correct word to complete each sentence and write the word in the space.

new, sound, take, only, little, work, know, place, year, live

rabbit   desk

1. Can you _____ this to him? only
                                            take

2. What was that new _____? place
                                          sound

3. I do not _____ what it is. know
                                            work

4. My desk is _____ this year. new
                                             only

5. What will _____ in this? year
                                          live

6. A little rabbit can get in this _____ little
    place.   work

Name _____ **Date** _____

Unit 11: JUST-FOR-FUN WORD SCRAMBLE

Directions: Unscramble the mixed-up words below. Write the correct word from the word box on each line.

| new, sound, take, only, little, work, know, place, year, live |

1. keta _____

2. kwor _____

3. lepca _____

4. enw _____

5. lyno _____

6. eilv _____

7. nusod _____

8. tiltel _____

9. arye _____

10. owkn _____

Unit 12: FLASHCARDS

Directions: Cut out the flashcards and use them to help you learn the words.

me, back, give, most, very, after, thing, our, just, name

me	after
back	thing
give	our
most	just
very	name

Unit 12: WRITE THE WORDS

Directions: Write the words in the spaces.

me, back, give, most, very, after, thing, our, just, name

me _____

1. _____

back _____

2. _____

give _____

3. _____

most _____

4. _____

very _____

5. _____

after _____

6. _____

thing _____

7. _____

our _____

8. _____

just _____

9. _____

name _____

10. _____

Name _____   **Date** _____

Unit 12: FIND THE WORDS—LEVEL A

Directions: There are 10 Instant Words hidden here.
Can you find and circle them?
Here are the words to look for:

after, give, me, name, thing, back, just, most, our, very

```
B  E  Y  W  A  S  V  Z
T  X  U  P  H  O  M  U
O  U  R  T  H  I  N  G
B  A  C  K  G  I  V  E
K  A  F  T  E  R  M  E
T  I  M  O  S  T  S  V
J  U  S  T  N  A  M  E
X  V  E  R  Y  E  N  W
```

Name _____ Date _____

Unit 12: MATCH PICTURES WITH SENTENCES—I

Directions: Draw a line from each picture to the sentence that tells about it.

back, give, thing, our, name

fly   dog   house

1.

   a. This is in back of our house.
   b. Our house is in the water.

2.

   a. Give it back to him.
   b. Give it back to her.

3.

   a. This thing can live in your house.
   b. This thing will fly by my house.

4.

   a. Write your name on this.
   b. What is the name of that dog?

5.

   a. You do not have to give it back.
   b. You can fly in this thing.

6.

   a. Our name is on our house.
   b. Give this to your dog.

Name _____   Date _____

Unit 12: MATCH PICTURES WITH SENTENCES—II

Directions: Draw a line from each picture to the sentence that tells about it.

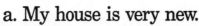

me, most, very, after, just

fly   house

1.    a. This thing can not fly after me.
       b. This thing will fly over our house.

2.    a. Many people can go in that.
       b. That thing is very long.

3.    a. Most people can fly in this.
       b. This is just for you.

4.    a. My house is very new.
       b. My house is after me!

5.    a. This is just a little thing.
       b. This is not very little.

6.    a. I can get to work just in time.
       b. I know most people fly these.

Unit 12: FIND THE WORDS—LEVEL B

Directions: There are 10 Instant Words hidden here.
Can you find and circle them?
Here are the words to look for:

after, give, me, name, thing, back, just, most, our, very

```
I  R  J  F  K  Y  X  H  G
O  M  D  U  R  M  A  S  I
M  U  O  D  S  E  F  B  V
Y  V  R  S  G  T  T  A  E
B  V  E  N  T  G  E  C  W
W  T  I  R  B  B  R  K  B
V  H  C  I  Y  Q  N  W  Q
T  K  V  W  B  Y  V  O  P
G  X  E  N  A  M  E  C  G
```

Name _____ Date _____

Unit 12: CHOOSE THE CORRECT WORDS

Directions: Choose the correct word to complete each sentence and write the word in the space.

| me, back, give, most, very, after, thing, our, just, name |

1. I can do my work _____ I do this. very
                                                                after

2. I like you the _____. most
                                                            just

3. That thing is not _____ long. very
                                                                   me

4.  I will write my _____. back
                                                            name

5.  Will you _____ this to her for me? thing
                                                                       give

6.  _____ name is on it. Just
                                                          Our

Unit 12: JUST-FOR-FUN MISSING LETTERS

Directions: The words on the basketballs are each missing a letter. Fill in the missing letters to spell the words from the word box. Then copy the completed words on the lines below the basketballs.

me, back, give, most, very, after, thing, our, just, name

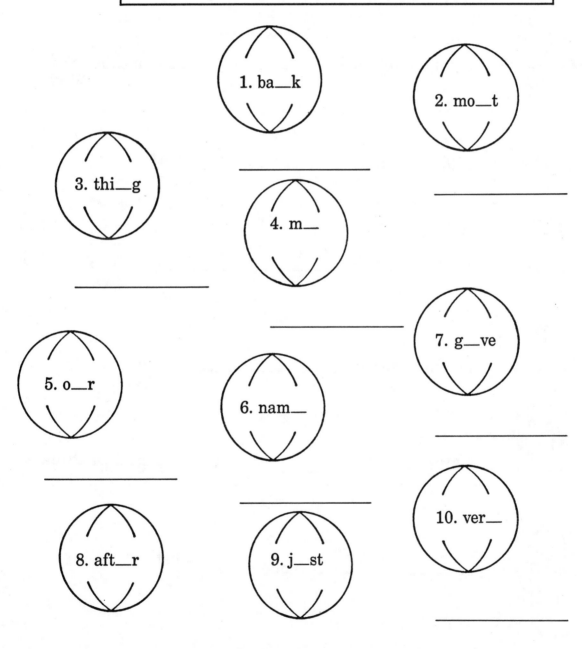

1. ba__k

2. mo__t

3. thi__g

4. m__

5. o__r

6. nam__

7. g__ve

8. aft__r

9. j__st

10. ver__

Name _____ Date _____

Unit 13: FLASHCARDS

Directions: Cut out the flashcards and use them to help you learn the words.

good, sentence, man, think, say, great, where, help, through, much

good	great
sentence	where
man	help
think	through
say	much

Unit 13: WRITE THE WORDS

Directions: Write the words in the spaces.

> good, sentence, man, think, say, great, where, help, through, much

good _____   great _____

1. _____   6. _____

sentence _____   where _____

2. _____   7. _____

man _____   help _____

3. _____   8. _____

think _____   through _____

4. _____   9. _____

say _____   much _____

5. _____   10. _____

Name _____   **Date** _____

Unit 13: FIND THE WORDS—LEVEL A

Directions: There are 10 Instant Words hidden here.
Can you find and circle them?
Here are the words to look for:

good, help, much, sentence, through, great, man, say, think, where

```
U  J  H  O  G  M  I  A  P  K  X
X  Q  G  F  D  Y  C  R  J  E  Y
V  B  E  S  N  S  R  Z  E  X  B
E  G  R  E  A  T  M  A  N  X  Z
S  A  Y  T  H  R  O  U  G  H  R
M  U  C  H  Q  G  O  O  D  B  U
S  E  N  T  E  N  C  E  B  M  H
H  E  L  P  N  W  H  E  R  E  A
U  C  W  B  I  I  A  M  M  H  M
I  T  H  I  N  K  T  Q  S  C  T
A  V  W  F  L  D  U  E  B  A  W
```

Unit 13: MATCH PICTURES WITH SENTENCES—I

Directions: Draw a line from each picture to the sentence that tells about it.

| good, sentence, think, where, help |

custodian   teacher

1.
   a. The teacher said, "That is a good sentence."
   b. Where did they go on that day?

2.
   a. I do not think I know you.
   b. The custodian can help you with that.

3.
   a. It is a good day to go there.
   b. You have to think when you do your work.

4.
   a. When did you write that sentence?
   b. Where did she go now?

5.
   a. I can help you with that thing.
   b. What do you think his name is?

6.
   a. Where were they then?
   b. You have been very good.

Name _____ Date _____

Unit 13: MATCH PICTURES WITH SENTENCES—II

Directions: Draw a line from each picture to the sentence that tells about it.

man, say, great, through, much

teacher

1.    a. We will have a great time.
   b. What did that man say?

2.   a. It is a great day to do this.
   b. It just went through there.

3.    a. How much is it?
   b. The people went through it.

4.   a. I will be a great man some day.
   b. What did you say?

5.    a. That is a great name for him.
   b. How much of that is for me?

6.   a. That man is my teacher.
   b. What did she say?

Unit 13: FIND THE WORDS—LEVEL B

Directions: There are 10 Instant Words hidden here.
Can you find and circle them?
Here are the words to look for:

great, man, say, think, where, good, help, much, sentence, through

```
H  W  Y  C  U  O  S  T  C  F  T  Z
O  W  N  C  R  D  G  F  H  Q  A  P
M  U  C  H  M  P  O  E  D  I  Q  H
U  E  M  H  A  J  O  Q  S  H  N  G
P  S  S  L  N  T  D  Y  G  A  M  K
C  N  E  C  W  E  M  U  G  O  Y  X
D  P  H  N  R  U  O  D  R  E  U  X
Z  W  K  E  T  R  J  W  E  C  K  P
K  R  H  X  H  E  F  U  A  O  H  X
Q  W  G  T  J  W  N  S  T  T  D  X
V  E  K  M  N  C  N  C  O  Y  M  G
H  E  L  P  X  P  X  U  E  J  F  T
```

Name _____ **Date** _____

Unit 13: CHOOSE THE CORRECT WORDS

Directions: Choose the correct word to complete each sentence and write the word in the space.

> good, sentence, man, think, say, great, where, help, through, much

1.  _____ did they all go? Where
   Help

2.  Are you all _____ with your work? think
   through

3.  I made a good _____ just now. great
   sentence

4.  How _____ can we give to them? much
   man

5. That is a _____ thing for you to do. through
   great

6. Did she _____ that you could come over? say
   good

Unit 13: JUST-FOR-FUN ANAGRAMS

Directions: Cut apart the letters on this page. Use the letters to spell each of the words in the word box.

good, sentence, man, think, say, great, where, help, through, much

a	c	d	e	e	e
g	h	i	k	l	m
n	n	o	o	p	r
s	t	u	w	y	☺

Name _____ **Date** _____

Unit 14: FLASHCARDS

Directions: Cut out the flashcards and use them to help you learn the words.

before, line, right, too, mean, old, any, same, tell, boy

before	old
line	any
right	same
too	tell
mean	boy

Unit 14: WRITE THE WORDS

Directions: Write the words in the spaces.

before, line, right, too, mean, old, any, same, tell, boy

before ———————————————— old ————————————————

1. ———————————————— 6. ————————————————

line ———————————————— any ————————————————

2. ———————————————— 7. ————————————————

right ———————————————— same ————————————————

3. ———————————————— 8. ————————————————

too ———————————————— tell ————————————————

4. ———————————————— 9. ————————————————

mean ———————————————— boy ————————————————

5. ———————————————— 10. ————————————————

© 1987 by Prentice-Hall, Inc. Fry's Instant Word Puzzles and Activities, E. Fry and L. Perry.

Name _____   Date _____

Unit 14: FIND THE WORDS—LEVEL A

Directions: There are 10 Instant Words hidden here.
Can you find and circle them?
Here are the words to look for:

before, line, old, same, too, any, boy, mean, right, tell

```
O  L  D  C  S  A  M  E  E
A  N  Y  F  A  M  E  A  N
B  O  Y  V  E  R  T  O  O
K  B  G  V  F  L  I  N  E
E  T  C  Y  V  V  Y  K  Z
B  F  C  A  I  I  Y  P  S
Y  E  T  E  L  L  O  Q  K
O  R  I  G  H  T  P  T  R
V  Y  L  B  E  F  O  R  E
```

Unit 14: MATCH PICTURES WITH SENTENCES—I

Directions: Draw a line from each picture to the sentence that tells about it.

line, too, old, tell, boy

girl

1.   a. The girl is in back of the boy in line.
    b. The old man will help them.

2.   a. Tell me how to write my name.
    b. It is too old to use now.

3.   a. The boy will tell you how to write a good sentence.
    b. The boy will tell you how to get there.

4.   a. That is too much for him.
    b. That is too old for him.

5.   a. She can not make a good line.
    b. She is too old to go there.

6.  a. Write your name on that line.
    b. Tell me what time it is.

Name _____ **Date** _____

Unit 14: MATCH PICTURES WITH SENTENCES—II

Directions: Draw a line from each picture to the sentence that tells about it.

| before, right, mean, any, same |

school

1.

    a. I do this before I go to school.
    b. We are right on time.

2.

    a. What did you mean for me to do?
    b. We were there before they were.

3.

    a. I will get in this line.
    b. I do not have any more.

4.

    a. Are these the same people?
    b. You are right about that.

5.

    a. We can use any that you have.
    b. He is very mean.

6.

    a. I will be there the same time as before.
    b. What did they mean by that?

Unit 14: FIND THE WORDS—LEVEL B

Directions: There are 10 Instant Words hidden here.
Can you find and circle them?
Here are the words to look for:

any, boy, mean, right, tell, before, line, old, same, too

```
T   H   M   K   H   W   N   H   T   B
G   W   E   I   W   R   V   G   R   O
X   B   A   O   L   D   Z   P   V   Y
U   Q   N   V   B   J   Z   X   E   N
D   B   A   A   G   K   G   M   K   T
M   E   R   H   S   G   A   N   Y   Z
F   F   I   I   M   S   E   N   W   Z
T   O   O   T   G   N   T   E   L   L
D   R   K   L   I   H   R   Z   X   A
E   E   H   L   L   P   T   P   Q   Q
```

Name _____   Date _____

Unit 14: CHOOSE THE CORRECT WORDS

Directions: Choose the correct word to complete each sentence and write the word in the space.

before, line, right, too, mean, old, any, same, tell, boy

1.  Have some of these _____ you go. same before

2. Do you think this is the _____ line? right before

3. They have the _____ name. same any

4. She is _____ little. old too

5. The boy did not _____ to do that. mean boy

6.  This is too _____. tell old

Unit 14: JUST-FOR-FUN WORD MAZES

Directions: Start at the arrow and trace over each maze to spell a word from the word box. Then copy the words on the lines below the mazes.

> before, line, right, too, mean, old, any, same, tell, boy

1.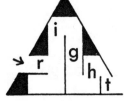

_____

2.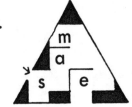

_____

3.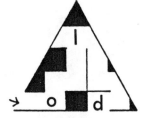

_____

4.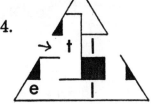

_____

5.

_____

6.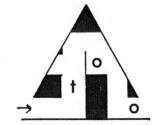

_____

7.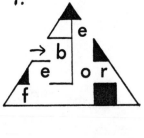

_____

8.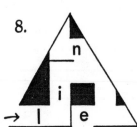

_____

9.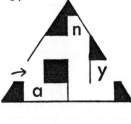

_____

10.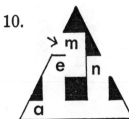

_____

Unit 15: FLASHCARDS

Directions: Cut out the flashcards and use them to help you learn the words.

follow, came, want, show, also, around, form, three, small, set

follow	around
came	form
want	three
show	small
also	set

Unit 15: WRITE THE WORDS

Directions: Write the words in the spaces.

follow, came, want, show, also, around, form, three, small, set

follow _____

1. _____

came _____

2. _____

want _____

3. _____

show _____

4. _____

also _____

5. _____

around _____

6. _____

form _____

7. _____

three _____

8. _____

small _____

9. _____

set _____

10. _____

Unit 15: FIND THE WORDS—LEVEL A

Directions: There are 10 Instant Words hidden here.
Can you find and circle them?
Here are the words to look for:

also, came, form, show, three, around, follow, set, small, want

```
S  E  T  C  A  M  E  B  B
P  S  H  O  W  G  S  Q  X
A  R  O  U  N  D  X  V  X
T  H  R  E  E  A  L  S  O
L  S  M  A  L  L  A  L  A
A  F  O  R  M  H  Z  R  T
M  X  T  K  I  W  P  N  M
U  I  G  F  O  L  L  O  W
I  W  V  N  W  A  N  T  H
```

Name _____ **Date** _____

Unit 15: MATCH PICTURES WITH SENTENCES—I

Directions: Draw a line from each picture to the sentence that tells about it.

came, show, form, three, small

teacher   bus driver   secretary   principal   custodian

1.   a. The teacher will show you where it is.
b. The teacher will help him form the number three.

2.    a. The secretary will show you what you need.
b. She came to the show with them.

3.    a. The principal will help the small boy.
b. The principal will show three of them how to get there.

4.    a. The bus driver came by to get her.
b. The bus driver can form that new word.

5.    a. All three of them will help.
b. The custodian will show you what time it is.

6.    a. They all came to see the show.
b. That form is very small.

Name _____ Date _____

Unit 15: MATCH PICTURES WITH SENTENCES—II

Directions: Draw a line from each picture to the sentence that tells about it.

> follow, want, also, around, set

draw

1.

   a. He can draw around that.
   b. I want to live in that.

2.

   a. They will want to go also.
   b. Now we have a new set.

3.

   a. She can use that set to draw.
   b. She will follow that line.

4.

   a. Did you follow what I said?
   b. All these people also live there.

5.

   a. They will go around and around.
   b. They will set that down right there.

6.

   a. I want to draw on that.
   b. They will follow her around.

Unit 15: FIND THE WORDS—LEVEL B

Directions: There are 10 Instant Words hidden here.
Can you find and circle them?
Here are the words to look for:

> also, came, form, show, three, around, follow, set, small, want

```
X  L  P  R  Y  E  L  V  E  M
L  J  Q  U  J  B  E  E  C  U
S  L  Z  P  Y  H  R  Z  E  W
H  S  W  N  W  H  I  I  D  I
O  M  L  A  T  A  J  A  D  N
W  A  U  V  R  A  N  Q  B  Y
U  L  Z  X  Y  O  L  T  C  K
U  L  C  A  M  E  U  S  Q  O
I  F  O  L  L  O  W  N  O  I
S  E  T  F  O  R  M  X  D  V
```

Name _____ Date _____

Unit 15: CHOOSE THE CORRECT WORDS

Directions: Choose the correct word to complete each sentence and write the word in the space.

follow, came, want, show, also, around, form, three, small, set

teacher   bus driver   secretary   principal   custodian

1.  Your teacher will _____ you how to do that. follow
   show

2. He may go _____ and around. around
    form

3. Our principal _____ by to see the boy. came
    want

4.  The bus driver will come by for all _____ of them. small
   three

5. 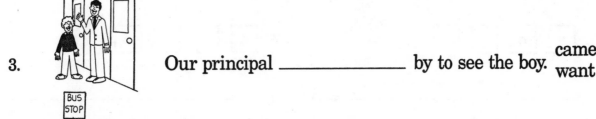 She just got a new _____ of them. set
   also

6. 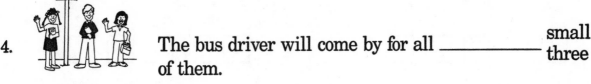 The custodian will not want him to _____ you. around
   follow

Unit 15: JUST-FOR-FUN LETTER SQUARES

Directions: Write the missing letters in the squares to spell the words from the word box. Then copy the completed words on the lines below the squares.

| follow, came, want, show, also, around, form, three, small, set |

1. | f | | | m |

   _____

2. | w | | | |

   _____

3. | s | h | | |

   _____

4. | t | h | | | |

   _____

5. | | e | |

   _____

6. | | | | | | d |

   _____

7. | c | | | |

   _____

8. | | | s | o |

   _____

9. | s | m | | | |

   _____

10. | | | l | l | | |

   _____

Unit 16: FLASHCARDS

Directions: Cut out the flashcards and use them to help you learn the words.

put, end, does, another, well, large, must, big, even, such

put	large
end	must
does	big
another	even
well	such

Unit 16: WRITE THE WORDS

Directions: Write the words in the spaces.

put, end, does, another, well, large, must, big, even, such

_put_____

1. _____

_end_____

2. _____

_does_____

3. _____

_another_____

4. _____

_well_____

5. _____

_large_____

6. _____

_must_____

7. _____

_big_____

8. _____

_even_____

9. _____

_such_____

10. _____

Name _____ **Date** _____

Unit 16: FIND THE WORDS—LEVEL A

Directions: There are 10 Instant Words hidden here.
Can you find and circle them?
Here are the words to look for:

another, does, even, must, such, big, end, large, put, well

```
A N O T H E R J Z P
G Z U W H S W K E R
L A R G E M U S T B
U H N C P U T E Z H
R O A Q H Z V I C S
A E U F O V D O E S
B I G X W E L L S C
G O H S K E V E N D
W X S U C H M G Q C
U X C O T X D P H A
```

Unit 16: MATCH PICTURES WITH SENTENCES—I

Directions: Draw a line from each picture to the sentence that tells about it.

put, another, large, big, such

shirt   pants   dress   shoes   hat

1.
   a. They all have on large shoes.
   b. They all have such little shoes.

2.
   a. She will put on another dress.
   b. She will put on another shirt.

3.
   a. He will write another sentence about a hat.
   b. He has on such a big hat.

4.
   a. Could you put his shirt on for me?
   b. You live in such a large place.

5.
   a. Put that water over there.
   b. We have had such a great time.

6.
   a. Another one was first in line.
   b. He has on very big pants.

Name _____ **Date** _____

Unit 16: MATCH PICTURES WITH SENTENCES—II

Directions: Draw a line from each picture to the sentence that tells about it.

> end, does, well, must, even

1.

    a. How do you think it will end?
    b. Does he know where you live?

2.

    a. They would not even give it back.
    b. We must get there on time.

3.

    a. The little boy is at the end of the line.
    b. The little boy said that sentence very well.

4.

    a. It is not even the right day.
    b. You must tell him when he does well.

5.

    a. He does not even know that word.
    b. He does that as well as some people.

6.

    a. I will get even with him for that.
    b. I must call to see if he can come.

Name _____ **Date** _____

Unit 16: FIND THE WORDS—LEVEL B

Directions: There are 10 Instant Words hidden here.
Can you find and circle them?
Here are the words to look for:

another, does, even, must, such, big, end, large, out, well

```
Y A N O T H E R G M P
P C G B B R D I D W S
P Y P G Y E B K U M D
H G D D E V E N A V H
S N C R O T L L O T U
E C M E S I L A U F M
A D F U S E Y P R L C
T Q M E W H X M F G W
S M O V C Q E F I R E
O D Y U H L I C R P P
V U S W Y N K X W M I
```

Unit 16: CHOOSE THE CORRECT WORDS

Directions: Choose the correct word to complete each sentence and write the word in the space.

> put, end, does, another, well, large, must, big, even, such

 shirt   pants   dress   shoes   hat

1. She can not put on such a _____ dress. even large

2.  He must get _____ hat. another does

3.  You must not tell me how it will _____. end well

4.  You have on _____ a big shirt! large such

5. She _____ not want such big shoes. put does

6.  You _____ be big before you can use these pants. must big

Unit 16: **JUST-FOR-FUN WORD SCRAMBLE**

Directions: Unscramble the mixed-up words below. Write the correct word from the word box on each line.

put, end, does, another, well, large, must, big, even, such

1. sutm _____

2. lewl _____

3. uhsc _____

4. oesd _____

5. nvee _____

6. henarot _____

7. gerla _____

8. utp _____

9. igb _____

10. nde _____

Name _____ **Date** _____

Unit 17: FLASHCARDS

Directions: Cut out the flashcards and use them to help you learn the words.

because, turn, here, why, ask, went, men, read, need, land

because	went
turn	men
here	read
why	need
ask	land

Unit 17: WRITE THE WORDS

Directions: Write the words in the spaces.

because, turn, here, why, ask, went, men, read, need, land

because _____   went _____

1. _____   6. _____

turn _____   men _____

2. _____   7. _____

here _____   read _____

3. _____   8. _____

why _____   need _____

4. _____   9. _____

ask _____   land _____

5. _____   10. _____

© 1987 by Prentice-Hall, Inc. Fry's Instant Word Puzzles and Activities, E. Fry and L. Perry.

Unit 17: FIND THE WORDS—LEVEL A

Directions: There are 10 Instant Words hidden here.
Can you find and circle them?
Here are the words to look for:

ask, here, men, read, went, because, land, need, turn, why

```
D  B  E  C  A  U  S  E  R  R
Y  C  T  U  R  N  E  E  D  O
J  O  X  N  M  E  N  C  T  O
H  Y  L  A  N  D  J  D  H  L
R  E  F  X  Q  M  R  O  H  G
I  L  K  P  D  G  C  N  P  L
X  P  B  E  A  S  K  T  R  S
T  U  Z  N  P  A  V  Y  L  C
X  W  H  Y  N  L  H  E  R  E
R  E  A  D  M  W  E  N  T  F
```

Name _____ **Date** _____

Unit 17: MATCH PICTURES WITH SENTENCES—I

Directions: Draw a line from each picture to the sentence that tells about it.

| turn, here, ask, read, need |

pen   pencil   crayon   typewriter   computer

1.

        a. It is my turn to use the computer.
        b. Ask them if they can find the computer.

2.

        a. Can you read this sentence about a pencil?
        b. I need another pencil.

3.

        a. Could you ask him to help us?
        b. He will need a large crayon here.

4.

        a. You can read what I write on this typewriter.
        b. It is her turn to follow the typewriter around.

5.

        a. Here is my new pen and pencil set.
        b. Ask the pen and pencil what time it is.

6.

        a. Is it your turn to use the computer?
        b. I need to ask the computer for more water.

Name _____ Date _____

Unit 17: MATCH PICTURES WITH SENTENCES—II

Directions: Draw a line from each picture to the sentence that tells about it.

> because, why, went, men, land

1.

   a. He went there to work.
   b. He is here because we are.

2.

   a. Why did the boy write that?
   b. He went there to see them.

3.

   a. These two men can do this.
   b. These men live on old land.

4.

   a. Why did she write on that line?
   b. I do not know why she is there.

5.

   a. It will not land here now.
   b. It went over the water.

6.

   a. We will get this because we need it.
   b. The men will like this new word.

Unit 17: FIND THE WORDS—LEVEL B

Directions: There are 10 Instant Words hidden here.
Can you find and circle them?
Here are the words to look for:

ask, here, men, read, went, because, land, need, turn, why

```
J   W   T   Z   R   N   T   A   D   I   P
O   B   E   C   A   U   S   E   E   Y   P
T   Q   F   N   T   C   E   F   I   V   G
B   W   S   T   T   N   R   Z   Q   A   Q
L   P   D   T   Q   Y   P   V   Y   B   H
W   A   S   O   G   Y   N   R   E   A   D
Y   H   D   E   I   R   A   S   E   C   I
Z   L   Y   E   U   L   S   R   T   O   K
S   Z   R   T   C   A   X   K   K   D   T
R   E   A   S   K   N   I   M   E   N   D
H   X   C   K   O   D   M   V   J   K   U
```

Name _____ Date _____

Unit 17: CHOOSE THE CORRECT WORDS

Directions: Choose the correct word to complete each sentence and write the word in the space.

| because, turn, here, why, ask, went, men, read, need, land |

pen   pencil   crayon   typewriter   computer

1. It it my _____ to use the typewriter. turn / land

2. I need a new pencil _____ I can not find my old one. ask / because

3. Who will _____ what I write on the computer? why / read

4.  These men work on the _____. land / here

5. I _____ another crayon. need / men

6. _____ her if we can use her pen. Ask / Went

Unit 17: JUST-FOR-FUN MISSING LETTERS

Directions: The words on the kites are each missing a letter. Fill in the missing
letters to spell the words from the word box. Then copy the completed
words on the lines below the kites.

> because, turn, here, why, ask, went, men, read, need, land

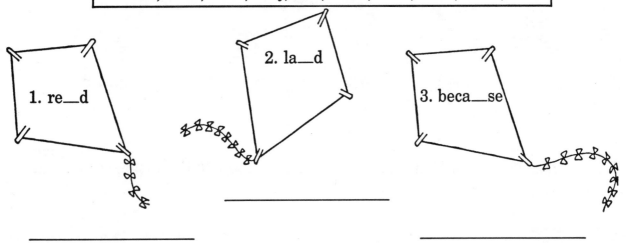

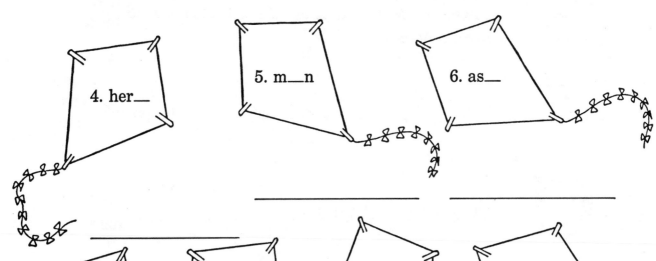

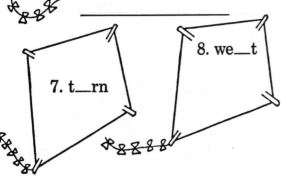

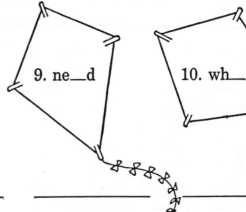

Name _____   Date _____

Unit 18: FLASHCARDS

Directions: Cut out the flashcards and use them to help you learn the words.

different, home, us, move, try, kind, hand, picture, again, change

different	kind
home	hand
us	picture
move	again
try	change

Unit 18: WRITE THE WORDS

Directions: Write the words in the spaces.

different, home, us, move, try, kind, hand, picture, again, change

different _____   kind _____

1. _____   6. _____

home _____   hand _____

2. _____   7. _____

us _____   picture _____

3. _____   8. _____

move _____   again _____

4. _____   9. _____

try _____   change _____

5. _____   10. _____

© 1987 by Prentice-Hall, Inc. *Fry's Instant Word Puzzles and Activities*, E. Fry and L. Perry.

Name _____ Date _____

Unit 18: FIND THE WORDS—LEVEL A

Directions: There are 10 Instant Words hidden here.
Can you find and circle them?
Here are the words to look for:

again, different, home, move, try, change, hand, kind, picture, us

```
T  E  L  V  G  B  M  O  V  E  Q  O
Q  G  Y  T  S  I  I  P  K  I  A  O
O  D  I  F  F  E  R  E  N  T  L  S
P  I  C  T  U  R  E  T  R  Y  Z  N
W  Y  T  F  W  L  Y  E  T  E  K  O
C  X  P  R  W  M  B  J  A  Z  W  X
R  R  N  V  G  I  S  B  H  K  E  A
S  B  M  X  C  H  A  N  G  E  U  S
Q  I  W  D  D  M  W  H  O  M  E  P
F  E  O  A  G  A  I  N  K  I  N  D
J  V  D  P  Q  H  A  N  D  O  J  R
O  K  Z  L  Y  D  H  R  H  N  N  G
```

Unit 18: MATCH PICTURES WITH SENTENCES—I

Directions: Draw a line from each picture to the sentence that tells about it.

home, move, try, hand, picture

elephant

giraffe

bear

tiger

monkey

1.
a. She has a hand like a giraffe.
b. She has a picture of a giraffe.

2.
a. The bear will try to read that sentence.
b. The bear is in his new home.

3.
a. We will move into our new home.
b. We will move our home up and down.

4.
a. That tiger will need to move over.
b. That tiger can live in my home.

5.
a. This monkey will try to say your name.
b. This monkey can use his hand like we do.

6.
a. The elephant will take a picture of you.
b. The elephant will try to get up on that.

Name _____ Date _____

Unit 18: MATCH PICTURES WITH SENTENCES—II

Directions: Draw a line from each picture to the sentence that tells about it.

different, us, kind, again, change

jump

1.

    a. Read this word again for me.
    b. Jump on this word again for me.

2.

    a. The people will change it for us.
    b. I need to think of a different sentence.

3.

    a. She will give these to us.
    b. She is very kind to these.

4.

    a. He will change that word to another word.
    b. He will jump on that with us.

5.

    a. What kind of thing is that?
    b. Do you want to change your name?

6.

    a. Will he jump over it again?
    b. I live in a different place now.

Name _____   Date _____

Unit 18: FIND THE WORDS—LEVEL B

Directions: There are 10 Instant Words hidden here.
Can you find and circle them?
Here are the words to look for:

again, different, home, move, try, change, hand, kind, picture, us

```
Y  Q  H  W  X  H  J  Y  Z  A  G  R  U
X  C  Y  S  Z  X  R  K  I  V  B  W  C
U  E  L  E  X  T  Q  H  C  J  C  W  O
P  A  E  U  D  K  J  Y  S  W  V  F  V
O  I  F  D  M  I  X  Q  R  D  R  S  F
H  D  C  D  D  L  F  K  I  N  D  L  L
O  K  U  T  P  S  T  F  A  G  A  I  N
M  A  O  J  U  U  S  P  E  T  F  C  E
E  H  A  N  D  R  M  X  T  R  F  H  O
Q  Z  M  O  V  E  E  V  A  M  E  A  B
V  O  K  B  L  V  A  J  U  Z  E  N  A
R  X  E  W  C  C  M  K  Y  Y  O  G  T
T  F  I  O  V  Q  V  J  I  C  V  E  C
```

Name _____ **Date** _____

Unit 18: CHOOSE THE CORRECT WORDS

Directions: Choose the correct word to complete each sentence and write the word in the space.

> different, home, us, move, try, kind, hand, picture, again, change

1.  The giraffe will need to move to a _____ home.

   different
   picture

2.  This man is very _____ to the elephant.

   home
   kind

3  The tiger will _____ to jump through it again.

   us
   try

4  She will _____ that picture for another one.

   kind
   change

5.  This bear will try to _____ in here.

   move
   change

6.  The monkey will try to _____ it to us.

   hand
   again

Unit 18: JUST-FOR-FUN WORD ANAGRAMS

Directions: Cut apart the letters on this page. Use the letters to spell each of the words in the word box.

different, home, us, move, try, kind, hand, picture, again, change

a	a	c	d	e	e
f	f	g	h	i	k
m	n	o	p	r	s
t	u	v	y	☺	☺

© 1987 by Prentice-Hall, Inc. Fry's Instant Word Puzzles and Activities, E. Fry and L. Barry

Name _____ **Date** _____

Unit 19: FLASHCARDS

Directions: Cut out the flashcards and use them to help you learn the words.

off, play, spell, air, away, animal, house, point, page, letter

off	animal
play	house
spell	point
air	page
away	letter

Name _____ **Date** _____

Unit 19: WRITE THE WORDS

Directions: Write the words in the spaces.

> off, play, spell, air, away, animal, house, point, page, letter

off _____

animal _____

1. _____

6. _____

play _____

house _____

2. _____

7. _____

spell _____

point _____

3. _____

8. _____

air _____

page _____

4. _____

9. _____

away _____

letter _____

5. _____

10. _____

Name _____ **Date** _____

Unit 19: FIND THE WORDS—LEVEL A

Directions: There are 10 Instant Words hidden here.
Can you find and circle them?
Here are the words to look for:

air, away, letter, page, point, animal, house, off, play, spell

```
S  I  H  O  U  S  E  O  C
L  E  T  T  E  R  M  D  X
C  V  W  L  N  N  T  P  O
P  O  F  F  N  L  B  U  D
A  W  A  Y  P  A  G  E  P
U  P  L  A  Y  C  P  V  I
S  P  E  L  L  A  I  R  T
A  N  I  M  A  L  H  W  E
X  P  O  I  N  T  M  U  J
```

Name _____ **Date** _____

Unit 19: MATCH PICTURES WITH SENTENCES—I

Directions: Draw a line from each picture to the sentence that tells about it.

off, play, away, animal, point

ball	doll	train	game	skateboard

1.
   a. That animal must get off my skateboard!
   b. That animal must not write with my skateboard.

2.
   a. See her take the doll away.
   b. See her point at the new doll.

3.
   a. They like to play their new game.
   b. The game will move off that place.

4.
   a. What kind of train is that?
   b. This train can play with us.

5.
   a. I see the animal point at the ball.
   b. I would like to play ball now.

6.
   a. We have to work before we play.
   b. Take that off and go away!

Unit 19: MATCH PICTURES WITH SENTENCES—II

Directions: Draw a line from each picture to the sentence that tells about it.

spell, air, house, page, letter

1.

a. The man will move to another house.
b. The man can go up in the air.

2.

a. Will you read this page to me?
b. Will you write this letter for me?

3.

a. She will live up in the air.
b. She will write a letter to some people.

4.

a. How do you spell your name?
b. All these people are in my house.

5.

a. Does he know how to spell that word?
b. What is that thing up in the air?

6.

a. Which page do you want to read?
b. He just went through the air again.

Unit 19: FIND THE WORDS—LEVEL B

Directions: There are 10 Instant Words hidden here.
Can you find and circle them?
Here are the words to look for:

| air, away, letter, page, point, animal, house, off, play, spell |

```
S  G  P  N  Q  J  W  R  M  B
A  W  B  A  M  I  W  A  E  U
L  W  P  J  M  P  I  I  C  A
M  E  A  O  F  F  P  R  S  N
P  L  T  Y  M  E  O  N  U  I
L  W  F  T  G  L  I  O  U  M
A  Z  G  A  E  Y  N  S  G  A
Y  B  P  B  F  R  T  X  Y  L
L  U  P  S  P  E  L  L  V  C
N  B  F  H  O  U  S  E  I  J
```

Name _____ Date _____

Unit 19: CHOOSE THE CORRECT WORDS

Directions: Choose the correct word to complete each sentence and write the word in the space.

off, play, spell, air, away, animal, house, point, page, letter

ball

doll

train

game

skateboard

1. Can we _____ ball at your house? play
point

2. This _____ can look like a doll. page
animal

3. The _____ came to him on a train. spell
letter

4. His skateboard is up in the _____. air
away

5. Turn it _____ after you play the game. off
page

6. We want this animal to go _____. away
house

Unit 19: JUST-FOR-FUN WORD MAZES

Directions: Start at the arrow and trace over each maze to spell a word from the
word box. Then copy the words on the lines below the mazes.

> off, play, spell, air, away, animal, house, point, page, letter

1.

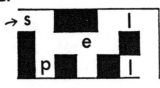

_____

2.

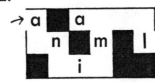

_____

3.

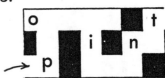

_____

4.

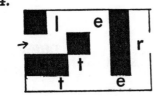

_____

5.

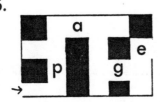

_____

6.

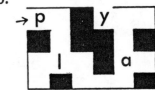

_____

7.

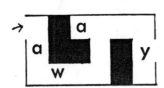

_____

8.

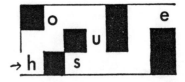

_____

9.

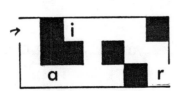

_____

10.

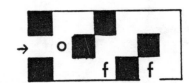

_____

Name _____ **Date** _____

Unit 20: FLASHCARDS

Directions: Cut out the flashcards and use them to help you learn the words.

mother, answer, found, study, still, learn, should, America, world, high

mother	learn
answer	should
found	America
study	world
still	high

Unit 20: WRITE THE WORDS

Directions: Write the words in the spaces.

mother, answer, found, study, still, learn, should, America, world, high

___mother_____   ___learn_____

1. _____   6. _____

___answer_____   ___should_____

2. _____   7. _____

___found_____   ___America_____

3. _____   8. _____

___study_____   ___world_____

4. _____   9. _____

___still_____   ___high_____

5. _____   10. _____

© 1987 by Prentice Hall, Inc. Fry's Instant Word Puzzles and Activities, E. Fry and L. Perry

© 1987 by Prentice-Hall, Inc. *Fry's Instant Word Puzzles and Activities*, E. Fry and L. Perry.

Name _____   **Date** _____

Unit 20: FIND THE WORDS—LEVEL A

Directions: There are 10 Instant Words hidden here.
Can you find and circle them?
Here are the words to look for:

America, found, learn, should, study, answer, high, mother, still, world

```
D  A  M  E  R  I  C  A  R  R
Y  M  O  T  H  E  R  C  O  J
O  X  N  C  F  O  U  N  D  T
S  T  U  D  Y  S  T  I  L  L
L  E  A  R  N  O  H  Y  J  D
H  L  R  E  F  X  Q  M  R  O
H  G  I  W  O  R  L  D  L  K
P  D  G  C  N  P  L  X  P  B
H  I  G  H  A  N  S  W  E  R
E  T  R  S  S  H  O  U  L  D
```

Name _____ **Date** _____

Unit 20: MATCH PICTURES WITH SENTENCES—I

Directions: Draw a line from each picture to the sentence that tells about it.

mother, answer, found, still, should

marker   scissors   paste   ruler   chalkboard

1.
   a. She will write the answer on the chalkboard.
   b. The chalkboard will write the answer.

2.
   a. My mother will still look for my scissors.
   b. My mother found my scissors.

3.
   a. Have you found the right answer?
   b. They should still be here.

4.
   a. I still have my old ruler.
   b. I have not found my ruler.

5.
   a. His mother said he could have that marker.
   b. His mother said he should be a marker.

6.
   a. My mother will get some more paste.
   b. My mother still has not found the paste.

Name _____ **Date** _____

Unit 20: MATCH PICTURES WITH SENTENCES—II

Directions: Draw a line from each picture to the sentence that tells about it.

| study, learn, America, world, high |

1.

    a. They live high up in the air.
    b. They will learn all about the world.

2.

    a. They will learn about America.
    b. There are no people in America.

3.

    a. They are high in the air.
    b. They can read and learn how to play that.

4.

    a. People all over the world know my name.
    b. They work and study there.

5.

    a. If we study a word we will learn how to spell it.
    b. That is too high for her to see.

6.

    a. See him study that sentence.
    b. He is from a different world.

Unit 20: FIND THE WORDS—LEVEL B

Directions: There are 10 Instant Words hidden here.
Can you find and circle them?
Here are the words to look for:

America, found, learn, should, study, answer, high, mother, still, world

```
K Y E L E A R N G Q Q
S V V H I G H C V A D
H A W V J T Z R N T A
O A I P O E Y P T C Q
U F O U N D F T I S W
L C F I V G B R W T O
D S T R Z Q E A Q U R
L P D T Q M Y P V D L
Y B H A A S O G Y Y D
S T I L L M O T H E R
Y D E A N S W E R I A
```

Name _____   **Date** _____

Unit 20: CHOOSE THE CORRECT WORDS

Directions: Choose the correct word to complete each sentence and write the word in the space.

mother, answer, found, study, still, learn, should, America, world, high

  marker   scissors   paste   ruler   chalkboard

1.  Her mother came to _____ when she was very little.   America answer

2. I _____ my ruler and my scissors, but not my marker.   found still

3.  We will study about the _____ we live in.   world learn

4. You _____ paste that picture right here.   high should

5.  We will _____ about America.   mother study

6.  You should write the _____ on the chalkboard.   answer high

Name _____ **Date** _____

Unit 20: JUST-FOR-FUN LETTER SQUARES

Directions: Write the missing letters in the squares to spell the words from the word box. Then copy the completed words on the lines below the squares.

mother, answer, found, study, still, learn, should, America, world, high

1. `f` □ □ □ □

_____

2. □ □ □ `l` `l`

_____

3. □ □ `t` `h` □ □

_____

4. □ □ □ □ `y`

_____

5. `s` `h` □ □ □ □

_____

6. `h` □ □ □

_____

7. `a` `n` □ □ □ □

_____

8. `l` □ □ □ □

_____

9. □ `o` `r` □ □

_____

10. □ □ □ □ □ `c` `a`

_____

© 1987 by Prentice-Hall, Inc. *Fry's Instant Word Puzzles and Activities,* E. Fry and L. Perry.

© 1987 by Prentice-Hall, Inc. *Fry's Instant Word Puzzles and Activities*, E. Fry and L. Perry.

Name _____ Date _____

Unit 21: FLASHCARDS

Directions: Cut out the flashcards and use them to help you learn the words.

every, near, add, food, between, own, below, country, plant, last

every	own
near	below
add	country
food	plant
between	last

Unit 21: WRITE THE WORDS

Directions: Write the words in the spaces.

| every, near, add, food, between, own, below, country, plant, last |

every _____

own _____

1. _____

6. _____

near _____

below _____

2. _____

7. _____

add _____

country _____

3. _____

8. _____

food _____

plant _____

4. _____

9. _____

between _____

last _____

5. _____

10. _____

Unit 21: FIND THE WORDS—LEVEL A

Directions: There are 10 Instant Words hidden here.
Can you find and circle them?
Here are the words to look for:

add, between, every, last, own, below, country, food, near, plant

```
L  A  S  T  U  O  E  L  M  I
B  E  T  W  E  E  N  D  S  P
Q  B  U  L  D  P  L  A  N  T
T  V  R  O  W  N  A  R  M  U
N  E  A  R  B  E  L  O  W  A
A  U  Q  A  D  D  J  I  R  B
F  O  O  D  E  V  E  R  Y  Q
U  T  E  L  V  G  B  Q  O  Q
G  Y  T  S  I  I  P  K  I  A
O  C  O  U  N  T  R  Y  O  L
```

Unit 21: WRITE THE WORDS IN SENTENCES—I

Directions: Choose a word from the word box to complete each sentence and write
the word in the space. More than one word from the word box may fit
some sentences.

every, between, below, plant, last

bush

flower

grass

corn

tomatoes

1. Not _____ plant has corn on it.

2. The grass is _____ the tomatoes.

3. The boy is _____ in line.

4. The letter is _____ the number.

5. He does not know where to _____ the bush.

6. The man is through with the grass at _____ .

7. There is a flower for _____ mother that is here.

8. The boy is _____ the corn.

9. My mother will help me _____ this bush.

10. The flower is _____ the corn.

Name _____ Date _____

Unit 21: WRITE THE WORDS IN SENTENCES—II

Directions: Choose a word from the word box to complete each sentence and write
the word in the space.

near, add, food, own, country

wash

1.   America is the _____ they live in.

2.   You have to wash that _____ before you can use it.

3.   Can you _____ one number to another number?

4.   He can write his _____ name.

5.   One house is very _____ the other house.

6.   She will just _____ a little of this to the food.

7.   You will like this new _____.

8.   He does his wash at a place _____ his house.

9.   They live a long way out in the _____.

10.   He can get his _____ food.

Unit 21: FIND THE WORDS—LEVEL B

Directions: There are 10 Instant Words hidden here.
Can you find and circle them?
Here are the words to look for:

below, country, food, near, plant, add, between, every, last, own

```
B  M  A  X  Q  P  O  W  N  I  W
D  D  M  D  W  P  L  F  E  O  J
V  D  P  Q  D  O  J  A  R  O  K
Z  B  L  Y  D  H  R  H  N  N  N
N  E  A  R  G  R  S  Y  N  T  S
Y  L  G  P  O  Y  R  E  D  D  D
M  O  X  W  R  T  E  K  D  O  M
L  W  V  E  N  W  H  L  O  P  J
K  D  V  U  T  T  H  F  A  E  G
L  E  O  E  K  F  B  P  O  S  T
W  C  B  N  A  U  A  O  L  Y  T
```

© 1987 by Prentice-Hall, Inc. *Fry's Instant Word Puzzles and Activities,* E. Fry and L. Perry.

Name _____ **Date** _____

Unit 21: CHOOSE THE CORRECT WORDS

Directions: Choose the correct word to complete each sentence and write the word in the space.

every, near, add, food, between, own, below, country, plant, last

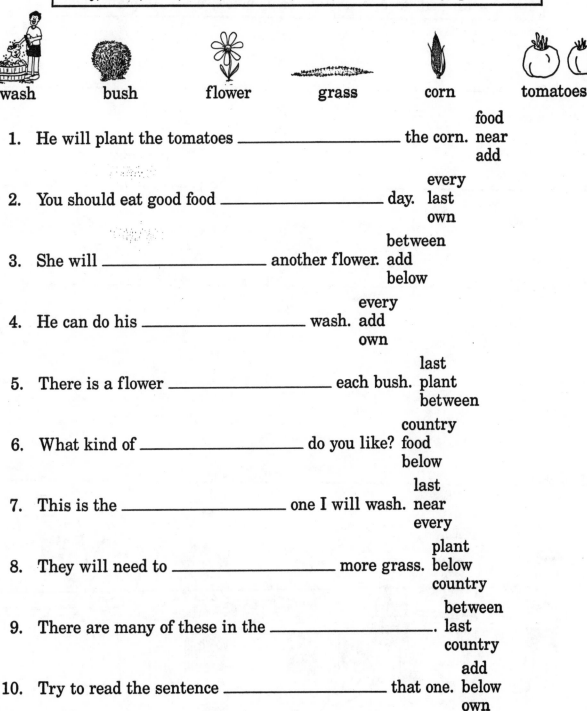

wash   bush   flower   grass   corn   tomatoes

1. He will plant the tomatoes _____ the corn.   food / near / add

2. You should eat good food _____ day.   every / last / own

3. She will _____ another flower.   between / add / below

4. He can do his _____ wash.   every / add / own

5. There is a flower _____ each bush.   last / plant / between

6. What kind of _____ do you like?   country / food / below

7. This is the _____ one I will wash.   last / near / every

8. They will need to _____ more grass.   plant / below / country

9. There are many of these in the _____.   between / last / country

10. Try to read the sentence _____ that one.   add / below / own

Unit 21: JUST-FOR-FUN WORD SCRAMBLE

Directions: Unscramble the mixed-up words below. Write the correct word from
the word box on each line.

> every, near, add, food, between, own, below, country, plant, last

1. tnlap _____

2. nwo _____

3. dda _____

4. odfo _____

5. wobel _____

6. veyre _____

7. wenebet _____

8. atsl _____

9. tuncyro _____

10. erna _____

© 1987 by Prentice-Hall, Inc. *Fry's Instant Word Puzzles and Activities,* E. Fry and L. Perry.

Unit 22: FLASHCARDS

Directions: Cut out the flashcards and use them to help you learn the words.

school, father, keep, tree, never, start, city, earth, eye, light

school	start
father	city
keep	earth
tree	eye
never	light

Unit 22: WRITE THE WORDS

Directions: Write the words in the spaces.

| school, father, keep, tree, never, start, city, earth, eye, light |

school _____   start _____

1. _____   6. _____

father _____   city _____

2. _____   7. _____

keep _____   earth _____

3. _____   8. _____

tree _____   eye _____

4. _____   9. _____

never _____   light _____

5. _____   10. _____

© 1987 by Prentice-Hall, Inc. Early English Student Word Power and Activities E, Fay and L. Fay

© 1987 by Prentice-Hall, Inc. Fry's Instant Word Puzzles and Activities, E. Fry and L. Perry.

Name _____   Date _____

Unit 22: FIND THE WORDS—LEVEL A

Directions: There are 10 Instant Words hidden here.
Can you find and circle them?
Here are the words to look for:

city, eye, keep, never, start, earth, father, light, school, tree

```
C  N  E  V  E  R  J  C  W
O  A  L  I  G  H  T  E  U
K  J  Y  S  C  H  O  O  L
S  F  A  T  H  E  R  W  V
C  I  T  Y  T  R  E  E  F
V  O  E  Y  E  F  D  M  X
Q  R  D  R  S  F  D  D  D
K  E  E  P  S  T  A  R  T
L  L  L  E  A  R  T  H  K
```

Unit 22: WRITE THE WORDS IN SENTENCES—I

Directions: Choose a word from the word box to complete each sentence and write the word in the space.

school, never, city, earth, light

sun   moon   star   cloud   rain

1. The _____ has only one moon.

2. Will you _____ this for me?

3. Do you think it will rain when we are at _____?

4. They go to this school in the _____.

5. You must _____ look right at the sun.

6. Many people live on the _____.

7. Their mother is from a large _____.

8. We get very little _____ from a star.

9. The sun was out when we went to _____.

10. I have _____ been on the moon.

Name _____   Date _____

Unit 22: WRITE THE WORDS IN SENTENCES—II

Directions: Choose a word from the word box to complete each sentence and write the word in the space.

| father, keep, tree, start, eye |

1. When should we _____ our work?

2. You should _____ away from this animal.

3. Put this over your right _____.

4. His father will plant this _____ for us.

5. It is your turn to _____ this at your house.

6. Ask your _____ to tell you the answer.

7. They all live in that small _____.

8. When did she _____ to follow you around?

9. Never get that near your _____.

10. They live in this house with their mother and _____.

Name _____   **Date** _____

Unit 22: FIND THE WORDS—LEVEL B

Directions: There are 10 Instant Words hidden here.
Can you find and circle them?
Here are the words to look for:

earth, father, light, school, tree, city, eye, keep, never, start

```
M K E Y Y O T F I O
V Y Q F N E V E R V
E J I C A V C M V H
G M D S A T T C T T
K E E P C R H R B Y
B M V X A H A E G T
D C I T Y E O Q R R
G F S N B E M O C E
Y J G L I G H T L E
T R I S I O C M D X
```

Name _____ **Date** _____

Unit 22: CHOOSE THE CORRECT WORDS

Directions: Choose the correct word to complete each sentence and write the word in the space.

school, father, keep, tree, never, start, city, earth, eye, light

sun   moon   star   cloud   rain

1. It may _____ to rain.
    light
    start
    keep

2. Some people went from the _____ to the moon.
    earth
    tree
    eye

3. This plant will need _____ from the sun.
    eye
    light
    earth

4. Our _____ will take us to school.
    city
    light
    father

5. This _____ is very large.
    never
    start
    tree

6. Do not get that in your _____.
    eye
    tree
    earth

7. There is a big cloud over their _____.
    school
    father
    start

8. People have _____ been to a star.
    earth
    never
    keep

9. They will move from the _____ to the country.
    school
    never
    city

10. You must _____ your hand away from this.
    father
    keep
    city

Name _____ **Date** _____

Unit 22: JUST-FOR-FUN MISSING LETTERS

Directions: The words on the shirts are each missing a letter. Fill in the missing letters to spell the words from the word box. Then copy the completed words on the lines below the shirts.

school, father, keep, tree, never, start, city, earth, eye, light

1. sc__ool

2. nev__r

3. st__rt

4. e__e

5. ke__p

6. fa__her

7. e__rth

8. t__ee

9. li__ht

10. cit__

Name _____ Date _____

Unit 23: FLASHCARDS

Directions: Cut out the flashcards and use them to help you learn the words.

thought, head, under, story, saw, left, don't, few, while, along

thought	left
head	don't
under	few
story	while
saw	along

Name _____ **Date** _____

Unit 23: WRITE THE WORDS

Directions: Write the words in the spaces.

thought, head, under, story, saw, left, don't, few, while, along

thought _____   left _____

1. _____   6. _____

head _____   don't _____

2. _____   7. _____

under _____   few _____

3. _____   8. _____

story _____   while _____

4. _____   9. _____

saw _____   along _____

5. _____   10. _____

Unit 23: FIND THE WORDS—LEVEL A

Directions: There are 10 Instant Words hidden here.
Can you find and circle them?
Here are the words to look for:

along, few, left, story, under, don't, head, saw, thought, while

```
G  M  Y  S  A  W  G  O  P  F
D  E  V  O  B  A  W  P  K  M
Q  Q  A  J  R  Y  D  O  N  T
O  P  G  D  W  J  F  E  W
I  G  B  J  C  C  I  E  K  S
G  P  N  U  N  D  E  R  Q  J
W  R  M  S  T  O  R  Y  B  W
B  A  W  H  I  L  E  M  I  W
L  E  F  T  H  O  U  G  H  T
A  L  O  N  G  H  E  A  D  E
```

Name _____ **Date** _____

Unit 23: WRITE THE WORDS IN SENTENCES—I

Directions: Choose a word from the word box to complete each sentence and write
the word in the space.

story, saw, left, few, along

cat   dog   rabbit   bird   fish

1. His father read him a _____ about a rabbit.

2. There are only a few fish _____.

3. She _____ their dog go after her cat.

4. Follow _____ and go where we go.

5. Only a _____ people were there.

6. I _____ three large fish go by.

7. She will write a _____ about a cat and a bird.

8. The boy only has one on his _____ hand.

9. Will you play _____ with us?

10. A _____ of them are still here.

Name _____ **Date** _____

Unit 23: WRITE THE WORDS IN SENTENCES—II

Directions: Choose a word from the word box to complete each sentence and write the word in the space.

thought, head, under, don't, while

sleep

1. She will want to sleep for a _____.

2. He _____ of a good story to read.

3. We _____ think we know this answer.

4. What is that thing on his _____?

5. They just went to sleep _____ it.

6. She _____ of a good place to play.

7. Don't put your head _____ there!

8. He put his _____ down and went to sleep.

9. _____ sleep too long.

10. You do that part _____ I do this part.

Unit 23: FIND THE WORDS—LEVEL B

Directions: There are 10 Instant Words hidden here.
Can you find and circle them?
Here are the words to look for:

| along, few, left, story, under, don't, head, saw, thought, while |

```
B  F  T  S  D  U  U  H  Q  K  B
H  H  T  Z  A  G  N  G  L  T  T
M  E  Y  H  N  W  D  K  C  M  F
H  R  A  O  O  E  E  Z  D  S  A
P  O  L  D  L  U  R  C  P  T  U
Q  A  U  I  G  F  G  G  O  O  Q
Y  U  H  S  U  C  E  H  T  R  F
A  W  B  X  A  A  T  N  T  Y  E
P  A  J  S  Y  J  O  D  A  P  W
L  K  R  Z  F  D  P  L  E  F  T
N  V  O  D  O  O  V  Z  T  P  D
```

Name _____ **Date** _____

Unit 23: CHOOSE THE CORRECT WORDS

Directions: Choose the correct word to complete each sentence and write the word in the space.

thought, head, under, story, saw, left, don't, few, while, along

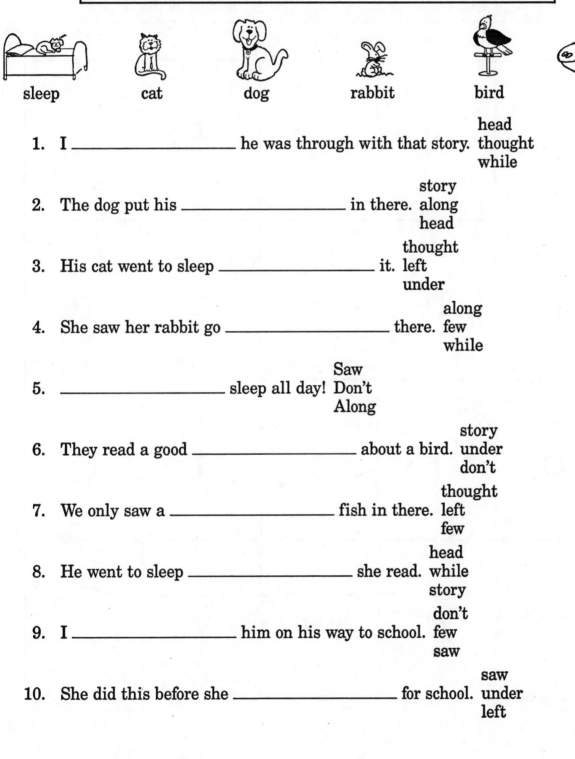

sleep   cat   dog   rabbit   bird   fish

1. I _____ he was through with that story. head / thought / while

2. The dog put his _____ in there. story / along / head

3. His cat went to sleep _____ it. thought / left / under

4. She saw her rabbit go _____ there. along / few / while

5. _____ sleep all day! Saw / Don't / Along

6. They read a good _____ about a bird. story / under / don't

7. We only saw a _____ fish in there. thought / left / few

8. He went to sleep _____ she read. head / while / story

9. I _____ him on his way to school. don't / few / saw

10. She did this before she _____ for school. saw / under / left

Unit 23: JUST-FOR-FUN ANAGRAMS

Directions: Cut apart the letters on this page. Use the letters to spell each of the words in the word box.

> thought, head, under, story, saw, left, don't, few, while, along

a	d̲	e	f	g
h	h	i	l	n̲
o	r	s	t	t
'	u̲	w	y	☺

Unit 24: FLASHCARDS

Directions: Cut out the flashcards and use them to help you learn the words.

might, close, something, seem, next, hard, open, example, begin, life

might	**hard**
close	**open**
something	**example**
seem	**begin**
next	**life**

Unit 24: WRITE THE WORDS

Directions: Write the words in the spaces.

might, close, something, seem, next, hard, open, example, begin, life

might _____

hard _____

1. _____

6. _____

close _____

open _____

2. _____

7. _____

something _____

example _____

3. _____

8. _____

seem _____

begin _____

4. _____

9. _____

next _____

life _____

5. _____

10. _____

Name _____   Date _____

Unit 24: FIND THE WORDS—LEVEL A

Directions: There are 10 Instant Words hidden here.
Can you find and circle them?
Here are the words to look for:

begin, example, life, next, seem, close, hard, might, open, something

```
L  M  I  G  H  T  Y  A  S  E  E  M
S  L  I  F  E  C  L  O  S  E  R  P
B  E  G  I  N  M  V  E  D  F  E  K
H  A  R  D  X  W  H  B  L  F  P  B
M  P  J  S  O  M  E  T  H  I  N  G
B  O  P  E  N  E  X  T  N  X  J  B
F  C  D  X  D  S  C  N  U  F  L  K
O  A  E  X  A  M  P  L  E  O  H  M
S  A  S  Q  Z  C  B  D  Z  F  L  J
F  Z  H  S  K  N  B  Y  Z  L  B  L
E  D  M  A  D  Y  W  I  H  N  H  B
X  R  E  V  J  Q  E  X  A  I  K  P
```

Name _____   **Date** _____

Unit 24: WRITE THE WORDS IN SENTENCES—I

Directions: Choose a word from the word box to complete each sentence and write the word in the space. More than one word from the word box may fit some sentences.

| might, close, something, hard, open |

farmer   police officer   cook   doctor   nurse

1. The cook will make _____ good for us.

2. This is hard to _____.

3. This is very _____ to close.

4. She _____ want to be a nurse some day.

5. A farmer has to work very _____.

6. They live _____ to us.

7. The police officer saw _____ move in there.

8. He can not _____ it.

9. The doctor said for him to keep his eye _____.

10. He _____ get this one right.

Name _____   **Date** _____

Unit 24: WRITE THE WORDS IN SENTENCES—II

Directions: Choose a word from the word box to complete each sentence and write the word in the space.

seem, next, example, begin, life

1. It does not _____ as if he is that old.

2. It is his turn _____.

3. This sentence is a good _____.

4. You may _____ work now.

5. He has a good _____.

6. It does not _____ that long.

7. You should do the _____ first.

8. When did this show _____?

9. The man is _____ in line.

10. She will write a story about her _____.

Unit 24: FIND THE WORDS—LEVEL B

Directions: There are 10 Instant Words hidden here.
Can you find and circle them?
Here are the words to look for:

close, hard, might, open, something, begin, example, life, next, seem

```
S  O  Y  G  Z  V  M  C  F  Q  X  E  Y
H  X  P  L  C  E  T  F  Y  C  Q  Q  W
U  P  Q  E  N  B  K  T  W  W  G  U  V
O  D  Z  M  N  C  E  G  R  N  F  L  L
T  U  S  P  P  A  C  X  I  Y  N  Z  L
S  E  E  M  F  D  T  H  A  I  V  S  B
N  F  P  X  V  R  T  C  G  M  C  W  E
C  L  O  S  E  E  E  V  M  P  K  W
F  V  D  A  M  L  B  P  Z  I  H  L  J
C  Z  J  O  Q  T  F  V  O  G  L  H  E
N  P  S  E  G  D  U  G  J  H  Y  A  H
N  E  X  T  L  I  F  E  X  T  J  R  N
N  W  J  S  J  L  Z  Q  A  N  D  D  S
```

Name _____ Date _____

Unit 24: CHOOSE THE CORRECT WORDS

Directions: Choose the correct word to complete each sentence and write the word in the space.

might, close, something, seem, next, hard, open, example, begin, life

farmer   police officer   cook   doctor   nurse

1. The boy _____ be a farmer when he is big.
                                                          might / life / hard

2. The doctor has _____ in his hand.
   open / close / something

3. Does he _____ mean to you?
   might / something / seem

4. The police officer will _____ the letter.
   open / next / example

5. These are very _____.
   begin / hard / something

6. They have a good _____ here.
   life / might / seem

7. What will the cook add _____?
   open / example / next

8. This _____ is different from the first one.
   close / example / hard

9. How did the show _____?
   begin / next / hard

10. A nurse is _____ if you need her.
   close / begin / seem

© 1987 by Prentice-Hall, Inc. *Fry's Instant Word Puzzles and Activities*, E. Fry and L. Perry.

Name _____ Date _____

Unit 24: JUST-FOR-FUN WORD MAZES

Directions: Start at the arrow and trace over each maze to spell a word from the word box. Then copy the words on the lines below the mazes.

| might, close, something, seem, next, hard, open, example, begin, life |

1.

_____

2.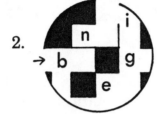

_____

3.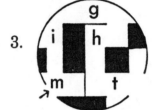

_____

4.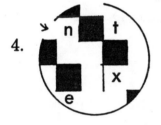

_____

5.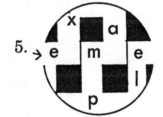

_____

6.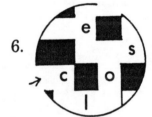

_____

7.

_____

8.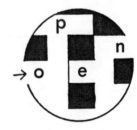

_____

9.

_____

10.

_____

Name _____ Date _____

Unit 25: FLASHCARDS

Directions: Cut out the flashcards and use them to help you learn the words.

always, those, both, paper, together, got, group, often, run, important

always	got
those	group
both	often
paper	run
together	important

Unit 25: WRITE THE WORDS

Directions: Write the words in the spaces.

| always, those, both, paper, together, got, group, often, run, important |

always _____   got _____

1. _____   6. _____

those _____   group _____

2. _____   7. _____

both _____   often _____

3. _____   8. _____

paper _____   run _____

4. _____   9. _____

together _____   important _____

5. _____   10. _____

Name _____ **Date** _____

Unit 25: FIND THE WORDS—LEVEL A

Directions: There are 10 Instant Words hidden here.
Can you find and circle them?
Here are the words to look for:

always, got, important, paper, those, both, group, often, run, together

```
D  I  M  P  O  R  T  A  N  T  R  R
Y  T  O  G  E  T  H  E  R  U  N  C
G  R  O  U  P  O  J  O  X  N  C  T
O  H  Y  J  D  H  L  R  E  F  X  Q
M  R  O  F  T  E  N  O  H  G  I  L
K  P  D  G  C  N  P  L  X  P  B  E
T  R  S  T  U  Z  N  P  A  V  Y  L
C  X  N  L  M  G  O  T  F  B  B  E
J  B  V  L  Q  M  Y  A  X  J  R  B
A  N  D  M  Q  I  U  F  A  L  K  Y
E  B  O  T  H  G  A  L  W  A  Y  S
P  A  P  E  R  Q  T  H  O  S  E  Q
```

Unit 25: WRITE THE WORDS IN SENTENCES—I

Directions: Choose a word from the word box to complete each sentence and write the word in the space.

both, group, often, run, important

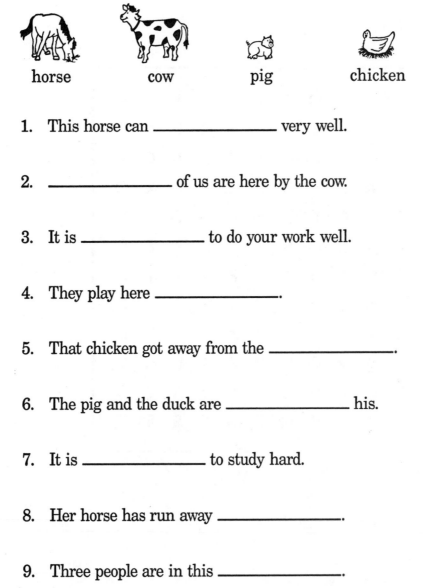

horse   cow   pig   chicken   duck

1. This horse can _____ very well.

2. _____ of us are here by the cow.

3. It is _____ to do your work well.

4. They play here _____.

5. That chicken got away from the _____.

6. The pig and the duck are _____ his.

7. It is _____ to study hard.

8. Her horse has run away _____.

9. Three people are in this _____.

10. He will try to _____ every day.

Name _____ **Date** _____

Unit 25: WRITE THE WORDS IN SENTENCES—II

Directions: Choose a word from the word box to complete each sentence and write the word in the space.

always, those, paper, together, got

1. Those two are always _____.

2. She has no more _____.

3. That animal is _____ near their house.

4. We need to help _____ people.

5. I want to read this _____ now.

6. What have you _____ in your hand?

7. I don't _____ know the right answer.

8. He can not put that thing _____.

9. Could I have some of _____?

10. What has he _____ under that?

Name _____   **Date** _____

Unit 25: FIND THE WORDS—LEVEL B

Directions: There are 10 Instant Words hidden here.
Can you find and circle them?
Here are the words to look for:

always, got, important, paper, those, both, group, often, run, together

```
R  L  P  D  T  T  O  G  E  T  H  E  R
Q  U  Y  P  V  Y  B  H  A  T  S  O  G
Y  Y  N  D  N  E  I  A  O  S  E  C  I
Z  L  S  E  R  T  O  B  K  S  Z  C  X
K  K  T  D  T  R  I  D  T  X  C  K  O
M  F  P  V  J  K  U  N  O  E  L  M  A
O  T  I  A  D  G  A  S  P  Q  B  U  L
L  D  H  T  P  T  R  V  R  A  R  M  W
U  A  A  O  R  E  U  O  G  Q  J  I  A
R  B  Q  O  S  U  R  T  U  O  E  L  Y
V  G  P  B  Q  E  O  Q  G  P  T  Y  S
T  M  S  I  I  P  K  I  A  O  O  L  S
I  Z  N  W  Y  T  F  W  L  Y  E  T  E
```

Name _____ **Date** _____

Unit 25: CHOOSE THE CORRECT WORDS

Directions: Choose the correct word to complete each sentence and write the word in the space.

always, those, both, paper, together, got, group, often, run, important

horse   cow   pig   chicken   duck

1. His horse and cow are always _____. run
    together
    often

2. How _____ do you see this show? often
    together
    group

3. This is an _____ day for him. always
    both
    important

4. That duck and chicken do not _____ much. those
    run
    often

5. She will put it in that _____. got
    paper
    those

6. His pig _____ out again! important
    paper
    got

7. I _____ do my school work first. always
    group
    both

8. They _____ like to read. both
    paper
    run

9. Are all _____ for us? got
    important
    those

10. This is a large _____ of people. together
    group
    always

Unit 25: JUST-FOR-FUN-LETTER SQUARES

Directions: Write the missing letters in the squares to spell the words from the word box. Then copy the completed words on the lines below the squares.

> always, those, both, paper, together, got, group, often, run, important

1. ☐ ☐ t h

_____

2. t h ☐ ☐ ☐

_____

3. ☐ o ☐

_____

4. a l ☐ ☐ ☐ ☐

_____

5. g r ☐ ☐ ☐

_____

6. ☐ u ☐

_____

7. ☐ ☐ ☐ e r

_____

8. o f ☐ ☐ ☐

_____

9. t o ☐ ☐ ☐ ☐ ☐

_____

10. ☐ ☐ ☐ ☐ ☐ ☐ ☐ t

_____

Name _____ Date _____

Unit 26: FLASHCARDS

Directions: Cut out the flashcards and use them to help you learn the words.

until, children, side, feet, car, mile, night, walk, white, sea

until	mile
children	night
side	walk
feet	white
car	sea

Unit 26: WRITE THE WORDS

Directions: Write the words in the spaces.

| until, children, side, feet, car, mile, night, walk, white, sea |

until _____

1. _____

children _____

2. _____

side _____

3. _____

feet _____

4. _____

car _____

5. _____

mile _____

6. _____

night _____

7. _____

walk _____

8. _____

white _____

9. _____

sea _____

10. _____

Unit 26: FIND THE WORDS—LEVEL A

Directions: There are 10 Instant Words hidden here.
Can you find and circle them?
Here are the words to look for:

| car, feet, night, side, walk, children, mile, sea, until, white |

```
C  A  R  Q  I  W  W  H  I  T  E
D  D  M  W  P  F  E  O  J  V  D
P  Q  O  J  R  O  K  Z  L  Y  D
W  A  L  K  H  M  I  L  E  R  H
N  N  G  R  S  S  Y  G  P  O  D
N  I  G  H  T  D  F  E  E  T  M
C  H  I  L  D  R  E  N  S  E  A
X  W  K  D  U  N  T  I  L  M  L
V  H  P  J  K  D  T  H  E  G  L
K  F  B  P  O  S  I  D  E  T  W
N  A  U  A  O  L  Y  Q  H  W  X
```

Unit 26: WRITE THE WORDS IN SENTENCES—I

Directions: Choose a word from the word box to complete each sentence and write the word in the space.

┌─────────────────────────────────────┐
│ until, car, mile, walk, sea │
└─────────────────────────────────────┘

bicycle   truck   bus   plane   boat

1. She had to _____ with her bicycle.

2. Will he go in a bus or a _____?

3. He had to walk a _____ to get there.

4. A boat can go in the _____.

5. We can not go home _____ it is time to go.

6. This animal does not like to ride in the _____.

7. They will _____ over to the big truck.

8. The plane is only one _____ up in the air.

9. These men will go in a boat on the _____.

10. We will not go _____ we see the light change.

© 1987 by Prentice-Hall, Inc. *Fry's Instant Word Puzzles and Activities*, E. Fry and L. Perry

Name _____   Date _____

Unit 26: WRITE THE WORDS IN SENTENCES—II

Directions: Choose a word from the word box to complete each sentence and write the word in the space.

children, side, feet, night, white

ride

1. These _____ want to ride all night.

2. Which _____ is he on?

3. We can only see these at _____.

4. The children have on something _____.

5. She will only write on one _____ of the paper.

6. What does he have on both of his _____?

7. The _____ like this new ride.

8. We keep this light on at _____.

9. Put these on your _____ when you go out.

10. The children live in a _____ house.

Unit 26: FIND THE WORDS—LEVEL B

Directions: There are 10 Instant Words hidden here.
Can you find and circle them?
Here are the words to look for:

---

car, feet, night, side, walk, children, mile, sea, until, white

---

```
F  V  O  F  M  D  M  X  K  Q  R  D
R  S  F  D  I  D  D  L  L  L  L  F
K  U  P  S  L  T  A  A  O  J  W  E
P  T  F  E  E  W  R  M  X  T  H  E
C  F  O  Q  Z  A  V  A  M  B  I  T
H  V  O  K  C  B  L  V  A  J  T  U
I  Z  E  A  R  X  E  U  W  C  E  C
L  M  K  Y  E  Y  O  T  N  T  F  I
D  O  S  D  V  Q  V  J  H  T  I  C
R  V  I  E  C  M  V  G  G  M  I  D
E  S  A  C  A  T  I  B  Y  B  M  L
N  V  X  G  D  N  Q  G  F  N  B  E
```

Name _____ Date _____

Unit 26: CHOOSE THE CORRECT WORDS

Directions: Choose the correct word to complete each sentence and write the word in the space.

until, children, side, feet, car, mile, night, walk, white, sea

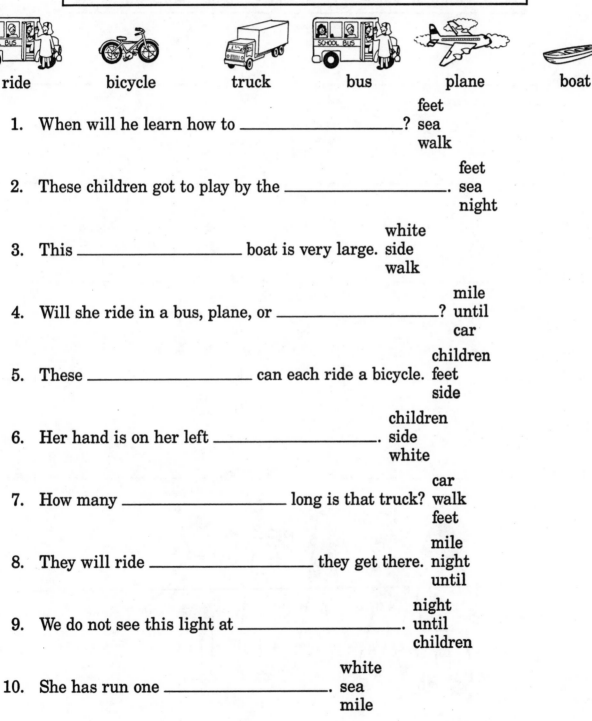

ride   bicycle   truck   bus   plane   boat

1. When will he learn how to _____?
    feet
    sea
    walk

2. These children got to play by the _____.
    feet
    sea
    night

3. This _____ boat is very large.
    white
    side
    walk

4. Will she ride in a bus, plane, or _____?
    mile
    until
    car

5. These _____ can each ride a bicycle.
    children
    feet
    side

6. Her hand is on her left _____.
    children
    side
    white

7. How many _____ long is that truck?
    car
    walk
    feet

8. They will ride _____ they get there.
    mile
    night
    until

9. We do not see this light at _____.
    night
    until
    children

10. She has run one _____.
    white
    sea
    mile

Unit 26: JUST-FOR-FUN WORD SCRAMBLE

Directions: Unscramble the mixed-up words below. Write the correct word from the word box on each line.

until, children, side, feet, car, mile, night, walk, white, sea

1. tefe _____

2. liem _____

3. hiwet _____

4. lutin _____

5. ase _____

6. drehinlc _____

7. ghint _____

8. acr _____

9. desi _____

10. alkw _____

Name _____ Date _____

Unit 27: FLASHCARDS

Directions: Cut out the flashcards and use them to help you learn the words.

began, grow, took, river, four, carry, state, once, book, hear

began	carry
grow	state
took	once
river	book
four	hear

Name _____ **Date** _____

Unit 27: WRITE THE WORDS

Directions: Write the words in the spaces.

| began, grow, took, river, four, carry, state, once, book, hear |

began _____   carry _____

1. _____   6. _____

grow _____   state _____

2. _____   7. _____

took _____   once _____

3. _____   8. _____

river _____   book _____

4. _____   9. _____

four _____   hear _____

5. _____   10. _____

Name _____   **Date** _____

Unit 27: FIND THE WORDS—LEVEL A

Directions: There are 10 Instant Words hidden here.
Can you find and circle them?
Here are the words to look for:

began, carry, grow, once, state, book, four, hear, river, took

```
P  U  C  B  E  G  A  N
P  V  R  I  V  E  R  I
T  H  C  A  R  R  Y  W
H  E  A  R  G  R  O  W
S  T  A  T  E  E  X  M
U  J  F  O  U  R  W  G
O  N  C  E  T  O  O  K
M  Y  B  O  O  K  G  O
```

Name _____   Date _____

Unit 27: WRITE THE WORDS IN SENTENCES—I

Directions: Choose a word from the word box to complete each sentence and write the word in the space.

took, four, carry, book, hear

      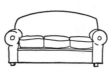

table   chair   sofa   chest   desk

1. Where will he _____ that chair?

2. The boy will read the _____ at his desk.

3. It _____ four men to carry the chest.

4. Do you _____ that sound?

5. There are _____ children on the sofa.

6. He _____ a good book to her.

7. The _____ is on the table.

8. She did not _____ what you said.

9. It is hard for her to _____ that table.

10. These _____ children walk to school together.

Name _____ **Date** _____

Unit 27: WRITE THE WORDS IN SENTENCES—II

Directions: Choose a word from the word box to complete each sentence and write the word in the space.

| began, grow, river, state, once |

sit

1. Which _____ does she live in?

2. The plant began to _____.

3. These children like to sit by the _____.

4. He went to this state _____.

5. We got there just as school _____.

6. These people _____ their own food.

7. This animal can sit in the _____.

8. They will move to another _____.

9. _____ you get there you will know where you are.

10. This is how the story _____.

Unit 27: FIND THE WORDS—LEVEL B

Directions: There are 10 Instant Words hidden here.
Can you find and circle them?
Here are the words to look for:

| began, carry, grow, once, state, book, four, hear, river, took |

```
W  R  M  B  R  O  N  C  E
B  E  G  A  N  I  W  B  F
A  S  C  M  I  W  V  E  O
H  U  T  A  P  J  M  E  U
P  E  I  A  R  C  M  B  R
S  L  A  M  T  R  N  O  W
U  W  F  R  L  E  Y  O  O
T  O  O  K  U  Z  R  K  G
T  S  G  B  B  G  F  X  Y
```

Unit 27: CHOOSE THE CORRECT WORDS

Directions: Choose the correct word to complete each sentence and write the word in the space.

began, grow, took, river, four, carry, state, once, book, hear

sit   table   chair   sofa   chest   desk

1. We are from this _____.
   river
   state
   book

2. Where will the men _____ that desk?
   carry
   grow
   once

3. They like to sit on the sofa and read a _____.
   four
   book
   near

4. All _____ of them can sit at the table.
   began
   carry
   four

5. This show _____ before I got here.
   once
   hear
   began

6. He can sit in an old chair by the _____.
   river
   four
   state

7. The plant began to _____ by the tree.
   took
   book
   grow

8. They _____ the chest in last.
   took
   state
   grow

9. We can not _____ her read.
   carry
   hear
   took

10. Come here at _____!
    began
    river
    once

Unit 27: JUST-FOR-FUN MISSING LETTERS

Directions: The words on the apples are each missing a letter. Fill in the missing letters to spell the words from the word box. Then copy the completed words on the lines below the apples.

began, grow, took, river, four, carry, state, once, book, hear

1. car__y

2. stat__

3. to__k

4. b__ok

5. riv__r

6. be__an

7. __nce

8. he__r

10. fo__r

9. gro__

Name _____ Date _____

Unit 28: FLASHCARDS

Directions: Cut out the flashcards and use them to help you learn the words.

| stop, without, second, late, miss, idea, enough, eat, face, watch |

stop	idea
without	enough
second	eat
late	face
miss	watch

Unit 28: WRITE THE WORDS

Directions: Write the words in the spaces.

> stop, without, second, late, miss, idea, enough, eat, face, watch

stop

idea

1. _____

6. _____

without

enough

2. _____

7. _____

second

eat

3. _____

8. _____

late

face

4. _____

9. _____

miss

watch

5. _____

10. _____

Unit 28: FIND THE WORDS—LEVEL A

Directions: There are 10 Instant Words hidden here.
Can you find and circle them?
Here are the words to look for:

eat, face, late, second, watch, enough, idea, miss, stop, without

```
C  M  S  E  C  O  N  D  F  H
R  E  N  O  U  G  H  E  A  T
Z  D  A  P  O  S  T  O  P  C
M  I  S  S  P  U  Q  U  G  F
G  O  Q  Y  U  S  U  C  E  A
B  X  A  A  T  P  A  J  S  Y
J  D  A  P  L  K  R  Z  F  P
N  V  W  I  T  H  O  U  T  O
L  A  T  E  D  W  A  T  C  H
O  I  D  E  A  F  A  C  E  O
```

Unit 28: WRITE THE WORDS IN SENTENCES—I

Directions: Choose a word from the word box to complete each sentence and write the word in the space. More than one word from the word box may fit some sentences.

> late, miss, enough, eat, watch

television   radio   movie   ballgame   band

1. They can _____ at the ballgame.

2. We do not want her to _____ school.

3. They will _____ a television show together.

4. This is a good movie for us to _____.

5. They have _____ people to form a band.

6. Did you get enough to _____?

7. We might be _____.

8. We will _____ them after they move away.

9. It is too _____ at night to turn on the radio.

10. Does the plant have _____ light and water?

Name _____ Date _____

Unit 28: WRITE THE WORDS IN SENTENCES—II

Directions: Choose a word from the word box to complete each sentence and write the word in the space.

| stop, without, second, idea, face |

listen

1. You must _____, look, and listen.

2. He can make his _____ look different.

3. They will all listen to his _____.

4. The plant will not grow _____ air.

5. She is the _____ one in line.

6. You must _____ that right now!

7. What does he have on his _____?

8. He was only there for a _____.

9. Don't go out _____ something on your feet.

10. She got her _____ from this book.

Name _____ Date _____

Unit 28: FIND THE WORDS—LEVEL B

Directions: There are 10 Instant Words hidden here.
Can you find and circle them?
Here are the words to look for:

eat, face, late, second, watch, enough, idea, miss, stop, without

Y O R J P W C B T E W
L U S S D N A A R U M
E B H E T N E Q G C I
N Y B V C O T R K W S
W J S Z W O P A E A S
T I E H R W N T Y T J
F J T N A J A D B C G
S A Y H O L W I V H R
P L C F O U I D E A T
U M O E H U G B H Q R
A Q D B R Y T H K Y Z

Name _____ **Date** _____

Unit 28: CHOOSE THE CORRECT WORDS

Directions: Choose the correct word to complete each sentence and write the word in the space.

| stop, without, second, late, miss, idea, enough, eat, face, watch |

listen   television   radio   movie   ballgame   band

1. He will _____ the late show on television.
   second
   idea
   watch

2. We will _____ and listen to the band.
   enough
   stop
   without

3. Does that watch have a _____ hand?
   second
   miss
   late

4. Your _____ is part of your head.
   face
   stop
   watch

5. They listen to the radio when they _____.
   face
   eat
   idea

6. I don't have _____ time to study all this.
   without
   miss
   enough

7. You might get an _____ if you listen.
   late
   second
   idea

8. I can not be _____ for my ballgame.
   late
   eat
   watch

9. They don't want to _____ any of the movie.
   eat
   enough
   miss

10. People can not live _____ air.
   stop
   without
   face

© 1987 by Prentice-Hall, Inc. *Fry's Instant Word Puzzles and Activities*, E. Fry and L. Perry.

Unit 28: JUST-FOR-FUN ANAGRAMS

Directions: Cut apart the letters on this page. Use the letters to spell each of the words in the word box.

stop, without, second, late, miss, idea, enough, eat, face, watch

a	c	<u>d</u>	e	f
g	h	i	l	m
<u>n</u>	o	<u>p</u>	s	s
t	t	<u>u</u>	w	☺

Unit 29: FLASHCARDS

Directions: Cut out the flashcards and use them to help you learn the words.

far, Indian, real, almost, let, above, girl, sometimes, mountain, cut

far	above
Indian	girl
real	sometimes
almost	mountain
let	cut

Unit 29: WRITE THE WORDS

Directions: Write the words in the spaces.

far, Indian, real, almost, let, above, girl, sometimes, mountain, cut

far _____   above _____

1. _____   6. _____

Indian _____   girl _____

2. _____   7. _____

real _____   sometimes _____

3. _____   8. _____

almost _____   mountain _____

4. _____   9. _____

let _____   cut _____

5. _____   10. _____

Unit 29: FIND THE WORDS—LEVEL A

Directions: There are 10 Instant Words hidden here.
Can you find and circle them?
Here are the words to look for:

above, cut, girl, let, real, almost, far, Indian, mountain, sometimes

```
Q  D  L  Z  I  Z  V  Y  H  J  M  K
G  X  B  P  M  A  B  O  V  E  M  M
H  I  N  D  I  A  N  F  A  R  Z  L
A  G  L  E  T  U  X  R  L  Y  E  P
M  C  T  H  M  Y  H  U  N  Q  O  H
P  O  K  P  Y  H  D  N  N  S  V  A
H  U  R  E  A  L  M  O  S  T  C  A
R  U  T  H  C  U  T  Q  V  U  Y  E
M  R  V  B  Y  X  L  A  C  F  Q  J
S  L  I  E  K  G  R  M  A  R  H  R
T  K  G  S  O  M  E  T  I  M  E  S
G  I  R  L  M  O  U  N  T  A  I  N
```

Unit 29: WRITE THE WORDS IN SENTENCES—I

Directions: Choose a word from the word box to complete each sentence and write the word in the space.

| Indian, let, above, girl, cut |

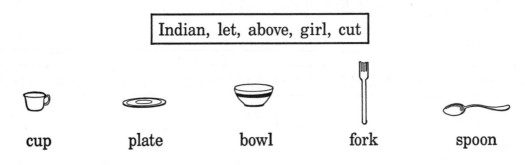

cup   plate   bowl   fork   spoon

1.   The girl will read a story about an _____.

2.   She will _____ him have that fork and spoon.

3.   This can go high _____ the earth.

4.   He can _____ that food on his plate.

5.   An _____ boy made this bowl.

6.   That little _____ can use a fork and spoon now.

7.   The cup is _____ the bowl.

8.   Do not _____ your hand with that.

9.   The little boy and _____ had the cup and plate.

10.   You may _____ him have that.

Name _____ Date _____

Unit 29: WRITE THE WORDS IN SENTENCES—II

Directions: Choose a word from the word box to complete each sentence and write
the word in the space.

┌───┐
│ far, real, almost, sometimes, mountain │
└───┘

laugh

1. _____ we laugh very hard.

2. They will go high up the _____.

3. How _____ have you read in that book?

4. That is not a _____ tree.

5. We can hear them laugh by the _____.

6. He is _____ as big as she is.

7. _____ they go to the river.

8. People can hear her laugh from _____ away.

9. It is _____ time to go home.

10. Is that a _____ watch?

Unit 29: FIND THE WORDS—LEVEL B

Directions: There are 10 Instant Words hidden here.
Can you find and circle them?
Here are the words to look for:

above, cut, girl, let, real, almost, far, Indian, mountain, sometimes

```
K  Z  A  P  M  B  C  Y  Q  B  Z  C  A
R  W  P  L  B  A  G  I  R  L  F  Y  H
X  Q  M  H  M  T  J  V  Q  T  Z  B  J
X  V  N  X  Y  O  E  H  U  I  G  W  B
K  D  J  K  S  M  S  C  D  H  T  Y  C
J  U  R  C  O  O  L  T  M  C  J  O  U
M  B  E  K  M  U  E  D  W  C  E  U  C
X  S  A  C  E  N  T  J  Z  U  J  N  I
U  W  L  C  T  T  Z  L  O  N  B  F  Z
W  J  L  N  I  A  Z  O  D  R  H  F  T
C  C  L  U  M  I  O  I  N  D  I  A  N
X  B  P  G  E  N  J  H  A  B  O  V  E
H  M  O  L  S  F  A  R  M  N  H  P  G
```

Name _____ **Date** _____

Unit 29: CHOOSE THE CORRECT WORDS

Directions: Choose the correct word to complete each sentence and write the word in the space.

far, Indian, real, almost, let, above, girl, sometimes, mountain, cut

| laugh | cup | plate | bowl | fork | spoon |

1. She _____ left her spoon in her bowl.
   - above
   - almost
   - girl

2. The little boy can _____ use a fork.
   - let
   - cut
   - sometimes

3. Did you hear the _____ laugh?
   - mountain
   - girl
   - almost

4. These men have run very _____.
   - sometimes
   - far
   - Indian

5. How far is it up that _____?
   - above
   - mountain
   - real

6. Put the cup _____ the plate.
   - far
   - girl
   - above

7. We can hear the _____ children laugh.
   - Indian
   - let
   - almost

8. It is hard to _____ through that.
   - far
   - real
   - cut

9. Are those his _____ feet?
   - Indian
   - real
   - sometimes

10. I will not _____ him get too far away.
    - let
    - cut
    - mountain

Unit 29: JUST-FOR-FUN WORD MAZES

Directions: Start at the arrow and trace over each maze to spell a word from the word box. Then copy the words on the lines below the mazes.

> far, Indian, real, almost, let, above, girl, sometimes, mountain, cut

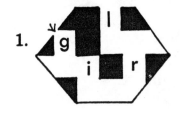
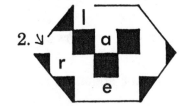

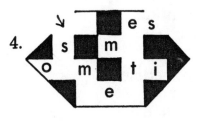
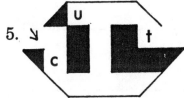

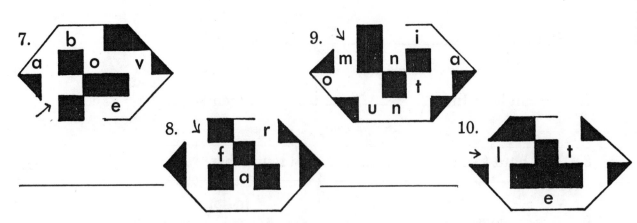

Unit 30: FLASHCARDS

Directions: Cut out the flashcards and use them to help you learn the words.

young, talk, soon, list, song, leave, family, body, music, color

young	leave
talk	family
soon	body
list	music
song	color

Name _____ **Date** _____

Unit 30: WRITE THE WORDS

Directions: Write the words in the spaces.

young, talk, soon, list, song, leave, family, body, music, color

young _____   leave _____

1. _____   6. _____

talk _____   family _____

2. _____   7. _____

soon _____   body _____

3. _____   8. _____

list _____   music _____

4. _____   9. _____

song _____   color _____

5. _____   10. _____

Name _____   Date _____

Unit 30: FIND THE WORDS—LEVEL A

Directions: There are 10 Instant Words hidden here.
Can you find and circle them?
Here are the words to look for:

body, family, list, song, talk, color, leave, music, soon, young

```
B   O   D   Y   S   O   N   G   H
O   M   U   S   I   C   M   E   N
A   Z   Y   F   O   G   Y   F   W
O   A   H   J   K   K   T   V   W
A   C   O   L   O   R   Y   H   G
U   T   W   F   A   M   I   L   Y
M   O   Y   O   U   N   G   W   Q
T   A   L   K   S   O   O   N   P
L   E   A   V   E   L   I   S   T
```

Name _____ **Date** _____

Unit 30: WRITE THE WORDS IN SENTENCES—I

Directions: Choose a word from the word box to complete each sentence and write the word in the space.

song, leave, family, music, color

store   gas station   church   theater   barn

1. She went to the store with her _____.

2. They will learn a new _____ in church.

3. What _____ is that barn?

4. She will play _____ at their church.

5. There are four people in this _____.

6. They will go to the theater after they _____ the gas station.

7. This gas station is the same _____ as a barn.

8. People play _____ at this theater.

9. When will he have to _____ that store?

10. They do not know a word of that _____.

Name _____ Date _____

Unit 30: WRITE THE WORDS IN SENTENCES—II

Directions: Choose a word from the word box to complete each sentence and write the word in the space.

| young, talk, soon, list, body |

sing

1. Don't _____ while people sing.

2. This food is good for your _____.

3. She is too _____ to talk.

4. His feet are too big for his _____.

5. She will write it down on her _____.

6. We think they will sing very _____.

7. Is he _____ or old?

8. Will she sing to us or _____ to us?

9. He said they would come see us very _____.

10. They will make a _____ of what they need.

Name _____ **Date** _____

Unit 30: FIND THE WORDS—LEVEL B

Directions: There are 10 Instant Words hidden here.
Can you find and circle them?
Here are the words to look for:

body, family, list, song, talk, color, leave, music, soon, young

```
K  Y  Y  L  S  H  U  O  R  U
S  I  H  Y  O  U  N  G  H  S
O  L  T  A  L  K  Z  S  H  C
N  S  E  Z  R  A  F  I  L  C
G  B  F  A  M  I  L  Y  I  O
P  I  O  A  V  N  O  S  S  L
G  D  T  D  O  E  U  R  T  O
D  E  K  O  Y  M  D  O  W  R
L  F  S  B  C  B  A  O  V  Y
T  E  C  C  Q  H  U  I  J  K
```

Name _____ Date _____

Unit 30: CHOOSE THE CORRECT WORDS

Directions: Choose the correct word to complete each sentence and write the word in the space.

> young, talk, soon, list, song, leave, family, body, music, color

sing

store

gas station

church

theater

barn

1. At the gas station they will work on the _____ of our car.
   song
   family
   body

2. The girl will sing a _____ at her church.
   song
   family
   list

3. There is a _____ boy at the barn.
   music
   body
   young

4. Don't _____ in the theater.
   song
   talk
   young

5. What kind of _____ does he sing to?
   leave
   music
   color

6. We need to go to the store _____.
   talk
   soon
   body

7. What did he write on his _____?
   list
   soon
   color

8. They like to sing with their _____.
   talk
   leave
   family

9. What _____ is the mountain?
   music
   young
   color

10. They don't want to _____ now.
    leave
    soon
    list

Unit 30: JUST-FOR-FUN LETTER SQUARES

Directions: Write the missing letters in the squares to spell the words from the word box. Then copy the completed words on the lines below the squares.

young, talk, soon, list, song, leave, family, body, music, color

1. ☐t ☐ ☐ ☐

_____

2. ☐s ☐ ☐ ☐g

_____

3. ☐ ☐e ☐a ☐ ☐

_____

4. ☐ ☐ ☐ ☐i ☐c

_____

5. ☐y ☐ ☐ ☐ ☐

_____

6. ☐b ☐ ☐ ☐y

_____

7. ☐ ☐o ☐o ☐

_____

8. ☐ ☐ ☐s ☐t

_____

9. ☐ ☐ ☐ ☐ ☐l ☐y

_____

10. ☐c ☐ ☐ ☐ ☐

_____

Unit 1: ANSWER KEY

Find the Words—Level A

Find the Words—Level B

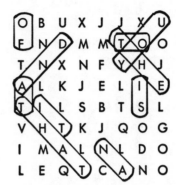

Match Sentences with Pictures—I

1. b
2. e
3. f

4. a
5. c
6. d

Match Sentences with Pictures—II

1. c
2. a
3. d

4. f
5. b
6. e

Choose the Correct Words

1. that
2. and
3. the

4. of
5. you
6. in

Just-for-Fun Word Scramble

1. is
2. that
3. the
4. it
5. a

6. of
7. and
8. in
9. you
10. to

Unit 2: ANSWER KEY

Find the Words—Level A

Find the Words—Level B

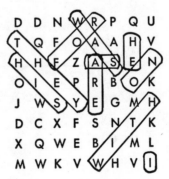

Match Sentences with Pictures—I

1. e	4. b
2. a	5. c
3. f	6. d

Choose the Correct Words

1. was	4. They
2. are	5. on
3. his	6. for

Match Sentences with Pictures—II

1. d	4. b
2. a	5. f
3. e	6. c

Just-for-Fun Missing Letters

1. with	6. as
2. for	7. they
3. his	8. I
4. he	9. was
5. are	10. on

Unit 3: ANSWER KEY

Find the Words—Level A

Find the Words—Level B

Match Sentences with Pictures—I

1. e	4. f
2. c	5. b
3. a	6. d

Choose the Correct Words

1. have	4. or
2. from	5. by
3. be	6. one

Match Sentences with Pictures—II

1. f	4. a
2. c	5. d
3. b	6. e

Just-for-Fun Anagrams

Answers will vary.

Unit 4: ANSWER KEY

Find the Words—Level A

WE S K CAN M
X R U X V B C Q
E A WHAT W D
NOT WERE T
Z YOUR Z O Z
SAID WHEN
S N O J H L J L
ALL I O BUT

Find the Words—Level B

Q L K N O R L F H
Q A L B U W G G W
I L I W Y WHEN
Y L L T E H Z U W
O S C W S A I D K
U B W A Q T E L S
R A U E NOT M R
D V V T R C V Y S
F S E T S E C E T

Match Sentences with Pictures—I

1. c	4. d
2. a	5. b
3. f	6. e

Match Sentences with Pictures—II

1. c	4. b
2. a	5. f
3. d	6. e

Choose the Correct Words

1. your	4. We
2. all	5. were
3. but	6. What

Just-for-Fun Word Mazes

1. what	6. your
2. when	7. but
3. said	8. we
4. were	9. not
5. can	10. all

Unit 5: ANSWER KEY

Find the Words—Level A

L THERE W X
R C J HOW U I
L X P WHICH
G E QUSE W W
SHE K H M A O
U F C F V A AN
THEIR F V
DO L EACH I

Find the Words—Level B

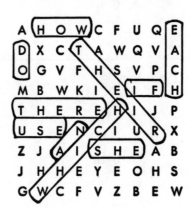

A HOW C F U Q E
D X C T A W Q V A
O G V F H S V P C
M B W K I E F H
THERE H I J P
USE N C I U R X
Z J A SHE A B
J H H E Y E O H S
G W C F V Z B E W

Match Sentences with Pictures—I

1. b	4. c
2. a	5. f
3. e	6. d

Choose the Correct Words

1. their	4. Each
2. Which	5. do
3. She	6. How

Match Sentences with Pictures—II

1. d	4. c
2. a	5. f
3. b	6. e

Just-for-Fun Letter Squares

1. their	6. each
2. she	7. use
3. an	8. do
4. which	9. if
5. there	10. how

Unit 6: ANSWER KEY

Find the Words—Level A

Find the Words—Level B

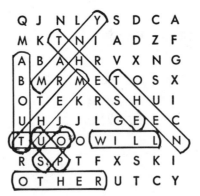

Match Sentences with Pictures—I

1. c	4. e
2. a	5. d
3. f	6. b

Choose the Correct Words

1. about	4. Many
2. These	5. So
3. them	6. other

Match Sentences with Pictures—II

1. d	4. b
2. e	5. f
3. c	6. a

Just-for-Fun Word Scramble

1. many	6. them
2. so	7. about
3. other	8. then
4. will	9. up
5. out	10. these

Unit 7: ANSWER KEY

Find the Words—Level A

```
T I M E  G H I X
G R Q G D G R L
L I K E  S O M E
H A S  U H E R  T
W L B  W O U L D
I  M A K E  L R V
Q  H I M  I N T O
L O O K  F N A P
```

Find the Words—Level B

```
R L U T K W L B I
L R V O H A S Q F
N A O P B T H E R
W L V A W X I D X
F O G F M W Y M E
Z Q U I L E S M E
K G H L K I O F H
E W E A D S K S X
Q F M I N T O E H
```

Match Sentences with Pictures—I

1. b	4. f
2. c	5. e
3. a	6. d

Match Sentences with Pictures—II

1. e	4. f
2. a	5. b
3. c	6. d

Choose the Correct Words

1. look	4. him
2. some	5. has
3. Would	6. time

Just-for-Fun Missing Letters

1. would	6. time
2. like	7. her
3. look	8. into
4. some	9. make
5. him	10. has

Unit 8: ANSWER KEY

Find the Words—Level A

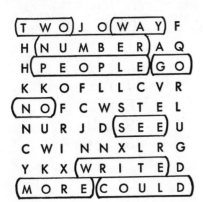

Find the Words—Level B

Match Sentences with Pictures—I

1. c	4. e
2. b	5. f
3. a	6. d

Choose the Correct Words

1. write	4. number
2. more	5. go
3. way	6. see

Match Sentences with Pictures—II

1. a	4. b
2. f	5. d
3. e	6. c

Just-for-Fun Anagrams

Answers will vary.

Unit 9: ANSWER KEY

Find the Words—Level A

```
Z J B E E N O W
C F I R S T E W
F S F I N D M Y
T W A T E R F V
U E T H A N P G
W H O C A L L Y
D O I L M L L U
X M V S Z Y K Z
```

Find the Words—Level B

Match Sentences with Pictures—I

1. d	4. e
2. c	5. b
3. a	6. f

Choose the Correct Words

1. first	4. been
2. My	5. find
3. oil	6. Who

Match Sentences with Pictures—II

1. c	4. a
2. d	5. b
3. f	6. e

Just-for-Fun Word Mazes

1. than	6. now
2. been	7. first
3. find	8. who
4. my	9. call
5. oil	10. water

Unit 10: ANSWER KEY

Find the Words—Level A

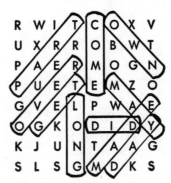

```
W S E L O N G
O V E R O W N
F D A Y D I D
M A Y J A I F
X C O M E N C
G E T P A R T
W B M A D E D
```

Find the Words—Level B

```
R W I T C O X V
U X R R O B W T
P A E R M O G N
P U E T E M Z O
G V E L P W A E
O G K O D I D Y
K J U N T A A G
S L S G M D K S
```

Match Sentences with Pictures—I

1. c		4. f	
2. e		5. a	
3. b		6. d	

Match Sentences with Pictures—II

1. b		4. f	
2. d		5. c	
3. e		6. a	

Choose the Correct Words

1. did	4. down
2. long	5. get
3. over	6. over

Just-for-Fun Letter Squares

1. did	6. may
2. made	7. over
3. long	8. get
4. down	9. part
5. day	10. come

Unit 11: ANSWER KEY

Find the Words—Level A

```
O N L Y I T A K E
N E W L I V E P I
Y Q U P K N O W W
D I P E N F D C D
U S O U N D A S N
N P L A C E H S I
W O R K Y E A R T
H L V W L G J C S
W H L I T T L E X
```

Find the Words—Level B

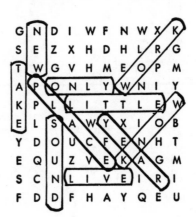

```
G N D I W F N W X K
S E Z X H D H L R G
T W G V H M E O P M
A P O N L Y W N I Y
K P L L I T T L E W
E L S A W Y X I O B
Y D O U C F E N H T
E Q U Z V E K A G M
S C N L I V E R I
F D D F H A Y Q E U
```

Match Pictures with Sentences—I

1. a	4. b
2. b	5. a
3. b	6. b

Choose the Correct Words

1. take	4. new
2. sound	5. live
3. know	6. little

Match Pictures with Sentences—II

1. a	4. a
2. b	5. b
3. b	6. b

Just-for-Fun Word Scramble

1. take	6. live
2. work	7. sound
3. place	8. little
4. new	9. year
5. only	10. know

Unit 12: ANSWER KEY

Find the Words—Level A

```
B E Y W A S V Z
T X U P H O M U
O U R T H I N G
B A C K G I V E
K A F T E R M E
T I M O S T S V
J U S T N A M E
X V E R Y E N W
```

Find the Words—Level B

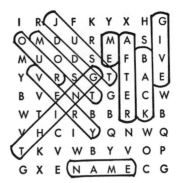

Match Pictures with Sentences—I

1. a	4. a
2. b	5. a
3. b	6. b

Choose the Correct Words

1. after	4. name
2. most	5. give
3. very	6. Our

Match Pictures with Sentences—II

1. a	4. a
2. b	5. b
3. b	6. a

Just-for-Fun Missing Letters

1. back	6. name
2. most	7. give
3. thing	8. after
4. me	9. just
5. our	10. very

Unit 13: ANSWER KEY

Find the Words—Level A

```
U J H O G M I A P K X
X Q G F D Y C R J E Y
V B E S N S R Z E X B
E  G R E A T  M A N  X Z
 S A Y  T H R O U G H  R
 M U C H  Q  G O O D  B U
 S E N T E N C E  B M H
 H E L P  N  W H E R E  A
U C W B I I A M M H M
I  T H I N K  T Q S C T
A V W F L D U E B A W
```

Find the Words—Level B

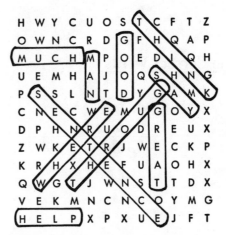

Match Pictures with Sentences—I

1. a	4. b
2. b	5. a
3. b	6. b

Match Sentences with Pictures—II

1. a	4. b
2. b	5. b
3. a	6. a

Choose the Correct Words

1. Where	4. much
2. through	5. great
3. sentence	6. say

Just-for-Fun Anagrams

Answers will vary.

Unit 14: ANSWER KEY

Find the Words—Level A

```
 O L D  C  S A M E  E
 A N Y  F A  M E A N
 B O Y  V E R  T O O
K B G V F  L I N E
E T C Y V V Y K Z
B F C A I I L P S
Y E  T E L L  O Q K
O  R I G H T  P T R
V Y L  B E F O R E
```

Find the Words—Level B

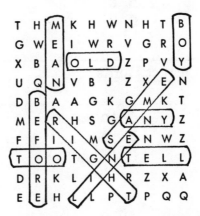

Match Pictures with Sentences—I

1. a   4. a
2. b   5. a
3. b   6. a

Choose the Correct Words

1. before   4. too
2. right   5. mean
3. same   6. old

Match Pictures with Sentences—II

1. a   4. a
2. a   5. b
3. b   6. a

Just-for-Fun Word Mazes

1. right   6. too
2. same   7. before
3. old   8. line
4. tell   9. any
5. boy   10. mean

Unit 15: ANSWER KEY

Find the Words—Level A

Find the Words—Level B

Match Pictures with Sentences—I

1. b   4. a
2. a   5. a
3. a   6. a

Match Pictures with Sentences—II

1. a   4. a
2. b   5. b
3. a   6. b

Choose the Correct Words

1. show   4. three
2. around   5. set
3. came   6. follow

Just-for-Fun Letter Squares

1. form   6. around
2. want   7. came
3. show   8. also
4. three   9. small
5. set   10. follow

Unit 16: ANSWER KEY

Find the Words—Level A

```
A N O T H E R  J  Z  P
G Z U W H S W K E R
L A R G E  M U S T  B
U H N C  P U T  E Z H
R O A Q H Z V I C S
A E U F O V  D O E S
B I G  X  W E L L  S C
G O H S K  E V E N  D
W X  S U C H  M G Q C
U X C O T X D P H A
```

Find the Words—Level B

```
Y  A N O T H E R  G M P
P C G B B R D I  D W S
P Y P G Y E B K U M D
H G D D  E V E N  A V H
S N C R O T I L O T U
E C M E S I L A U F M
A D F U S E Y P R L C
T Q M E W H X M F G W
S M O V C Q E F I R E
O D Y U H L I C R P P
V U S W Y N K X W M I
```

Match Pictures with Sentences—I

1. a	4. b
2. a	5. b
3. b	6. b

Match Pictures with Sentences—II

1. a	4. b
2. b	5. b
3. a	6. b

Choose the Correct Words

1. large	4. such
2. another	5. does
3. end	6. must

Just-for-Fun Word Scramble

1. must	6. another
2. well	7. large
3. such	8. put
4. does	9. big
5. even	10. end

Unit 17: ANSWER KEY

Find the Words—Level A

```
D  B E C A U S E  R R
Y C  T U R  N E E D  O
J O X N  M E N  C T O
H Y  L A N D  J D H L
R E F X Q M R O H G
I L K P D G C N P L
X P B E  A S K  T R S
T U Z N P A V Y L C
X  W H Y  N L  H E R E
R E A D  M  W E N T  F
```

Find the Words—Level B

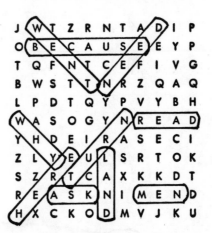

```
J  W T Z R N T A D I P
O  B E C A U S E  E Y P
T Q F N T C E F I V G
B W S T T N R Z Q A Q
L P D T Q Y P V Y B H
W A S O G Y N  R E A D
Y H D E I R A S E C I
Z L Y E U L S R T O K
S Z R T C A X K K D T
R E A S K N I  M E N  D
H X C K O D M V J K U
```

251

Match Pictures with Sentences—I

1. a
2. b
3. a
4. a
5. a
6. a

Match Pictures with Sentences—II

1. b
2. b
3. a
4. b
5. a
6. a

Choose the Correct Words

1. turn
2. because
3. read
4. land
5. need
6. Ask

Just-for-Fun Missing Letters

1. read
2. land
3. because
4. here
5. men
6. ask
7. turn
8. went
9. need
10. why

Unit 18: ANSWER KEY

Find the Words—Level A

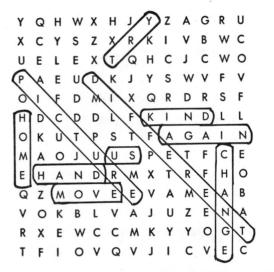

```
T E L V G B M O V E Q O
Q G Y T S I I P K I A O
O D I F F E R E N T L S
P I C T U R E T R Y Z N
W Y T F W L Y E T E K O
C X P R W M B J A Z W X
R R N V G I S B H K E A
S B M X C H A N G E U S
Q I W D D M W H O M E P
F E O A G A I N K I N D
J V D P Q H A N D O J R
O K Z L Y D H R H N N G
```

Find the Words—Level B

```
Y Q H W X H J Y Z A G R U
X C Y S Z X R K I V B W C
U E L E X T Q H C J C W O
P A E U D K J Y S W V F V
O I F D M I X Q R D R S F
H D C D D L F K I N D L L
O K U T P S T F A G A I N
M A O J U U S P E T F C E
E H A N D R M X T R F H O
Q Z M O V E E V A M E A B
V O K B L V A J U Z E N A
R X E W C C M K Y Y O G T
T F I O V Q V J I C V E C
```

Match Pictures with Sentences—I

1. b
2. b
3. a
4. a
5. b
6. b

Match Pictures with Sentences—II

1. a
2. b
3. a
4. a
5. a
6. a

Choose the Correct Words

1. different
2. kind
3. try
4. change
5. move
6. hand

Just-for-Fun Anagrams

Answers will vary.

Unit 19: ANSWER KEY

Find the Words—Level A

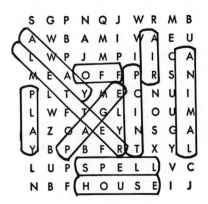

Find the Words—Level B

Match Pictures with Sentences—I

1. a	4. a
2. b	5. b
3. a	6. b

Match Pictures with Sentences—II

1. a	4. a
2. a	5. b
3. b	6. a

Choose the Correct Words

1. play	4. air
2. animal	5. off
3. letter	6. away

Just-for-Fun Word Mazes

1. spell	6. play
2. animal	7. away
3. point	8. house
4. letter	9. air
5. page	10. off

Unit 20: ANSWER KEY

Find the Words—Level A

Find the Words—Level B

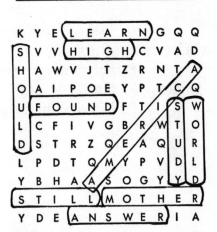

Match Pictures with Sentences—I

1. a	4. a
2. b	5. a
3. a	6. a

Choose the Correct Words

1. America	4. should
2. found	5. study
3. world	6. answer

Match Pictures with Sentences—II

1. b	4. b
2. a	5. a
3. b	6. b

Just-for-Fun Letter Squares

1. found	6. high
2. still	7. answer
3. mother	8. learn
4. study	9. world
5. should	10. America

Unit 21: ANSWER KEY

Find the Words—Level A

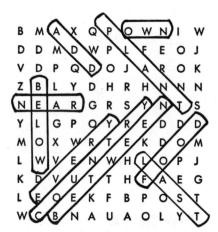

Find the Words—Level B

Write the Words in Sentences—I

1. every	6. last
2. between/below	7. every
3. last	8. between
4. below/between	9. plant
5. plant	10. between/below

Write the Words in Sentences—II

1. country	6. add
2. food	7. food
3. add	8. near
4. own	9. country
5. near	10. own

Choose the Correct Words

1. near	6. food
2. every	7. last
3. add	8. plant
4. own	9. country
5. between	10. below

Just-for-Fun Word Scramble

1. plant	6. every
2. own	7. between
3. add	8. last
4. food	9. country
5. below	10. near

Unit 22: ANSWER KEY

Find the Words—Level A

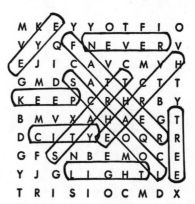

Find the Words—Level B

Write the Words in Sentences—I

1. earth	6. earth
2. light	7. city
3. school	8. light
4. city	9. school
5. never	10. never

Write the Words in Sentences—II

1. start	6. father
2. keep	7. tree
3. eye	8. start
4. tree	9. eye
5. keep	10. father

Choose the Correct Words

1. start	6. eye
2. earth	7. school
3. light	8. never
4. father	9. city
5. tree	10. keep

Just-for-Fun Missing Letters

1. school	6. father
2. never	7. earth
3. start	8. tree
4. eye	9. light
5. keep	10. city

Unit 23: ANSWER KEY

Find the Words—Level A

```
G M Y (S A W) G O P F
D E V O B A W P K M
Q Q A J R Y (D O N T)
O P G D W V J (F E W)
I G B J C C I E K S
G P N (U N D E R) Q J
W R M (S T O R Y) B W
B A (W H I L E) M I W
(L E F T) H O U G H T)
(A L O N G) H E A D E)
```

Find the Words—Level B

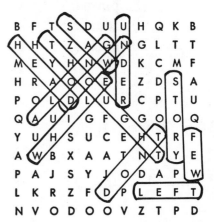

Write the Words in Sentences—I

1. story	6. saw
2. left	7. story
3. saw	8. left
4. along	9. along
5. few	10. few

Write the Words in Sentences—II

1. while	6. thought
2. thought	7. under
3. don't	8. head
4. head	9. Don't
5. under	10. while

Choose the Correct Words

1. thought	6. story
2. head	7. few
3. under	8. while
4. along	9. saw
5. Don't	10. left

Just-for-Fun Anagrams

Answers will vary.

Unit 24: ANSWER KEY

Find the Words—Level A

```
L  M I G H T  Y A  S E E M
S  L I F E  C L O S E  R P
B E G I N  M V E D F E K
H A R D  X W H B L F P B
M P J  S O M E T H I N G
B  O P E  N E X T  N X J B
F C D X D S C N U F L K
O A  E X A M P L E  O H M
S A S Q Z C B D Z F L J
F Z H S K N B Y Z L B L
E D M A D Y W I H N H B
X R E V J Q E X A I K P
```

Find the Words—Level B

```
S  O Y G Z V M C F Q X E Y
H X P L C E T F Y C Q Q W
U P Q E N B K T W W G U V
O D Z M N C E G R N F L L
T U S P P A C X Y N Z L L
S E E M  F D T H A I V S B
N F P X V R T C G M C W E
C L O S E  E E E M P K W
F V D A M L B P Z I H L J
C Z J O Q T F V O G L H E
N P S E G D U G J H Y A H
N E X T  L I F E  X T J R N
N W J S J L Z Q A N D D S
```

Write the Words in Sentences—I

1. something
2. open/close
3. hard
4. might
5. hard

6. close
7. something
8. close/open
9. open
10. might

Write the Words in Sentences—II

1. seem
2. next
3. example
4. begin
5. life

6. seem
7. example
8. begin
9. next
10. life

Choose the Correct Words

1. might
2. something
3. seem
4. open
5. hard

6. life
7. next
8. example
9. begin
10. close

Just-for-Fun Word Mazes

1. something
2. begin
3. might
4. next
5. example

6. close
7. hard
8. open
9. life
10. seem

Unit 25: ANSWER KEY

Find the Words—Level A

```
D I M P O R T A N T R R
Y T O G E T H E R U N C
G R O U P O J O X N C T
O H Y J D H L R E F X Q
M R O F T E N O H G I L
K P D G C N P L X P B E
T R S T U Z N P A V Y L
C X N L M G O T F B B E
J B V L Q M Y A X J R B
A N D M Q I U F A L K Y
E B O T H G A L W A Y S
P A P E R Q T H O S E Q
```

Find the Words—Level B

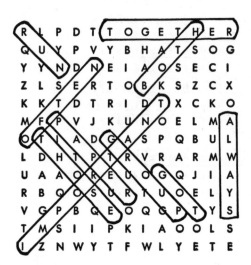

Write the Words in Sentences—I

1. run	6. both
2. Both	7. important
3. important	8. often
4. often	9. group
5. group	10. run

Write the Words in Sentences—II

1. together	6. got
2. paper	7. always
3. always	8. together
4. those	9. those
5. paper	10. got

Choose the Correct Words

1. together	6. got
2. Both	7. important
3. important	8. both
4. run	9. those
5. paper	10. group

Just-for-Fun Letter Squares

1. both	6. run
2. those	7. paper
3. got	8. often
4. always	9. together
5. group	10. important

Unit 26: ANSWER KEY

Find the Words—Level A

```
C A R  Q I W  W H I T E
D D M W P F E O J V D
P Q O J R O K Z L Y D
W A L K  H  M I L E  R H
N N G R S S Y G P O D
N I G H T  D  F E E T  M
C H I L D R E N  S E A
X W K D  U N T I L  M L
V H P J K D T H E G L
K F B P O  S I D E  T W
N A U A O L Y Q H W X
```

Find the Words—Level B

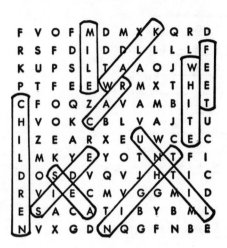

Write the Words in Sentences—I

1. walk
2. car
3. mile
4. sea
5. until
6. car
7. walk
8. mile
9. sea
10. until

Write the Words in Sentences—II

1. children
2. side
3. night
4. white
5. side
6. feet
7. children
8. night
9. feet
10. white

Choose the Correct Words

1. walk
2. sea
3. white
4. car
5. children
6. side
7. feet
8. until
9. night
10. mile

Just-for-Fun Word Scramble

1. left
2. mile
3. white
4. until
5. sea
6. children
7. night
8. car
9. side
10. walk

259

Unit 27: ANSWER KEY

Find the Words—Level A

```
P U C B E G A N
P V R I V E R I
T H C A R R Y W
H E A R G R O W
S T A T E E X M
U J F O U R W G
O N C E T O O K
M Y B O O K G O
```

Find the Words—Level B

```
W R M B R O N C E
B E G A N I W B F
A S C M I W V E O
H U T A P J M E U
P E I A R C M B R
S L A M T R N O W
U W F R L E Y O O
T O O K U Z R K G
T S G B B G F X Y
```

Write the Words in Sentences—I

1. carry	6. took
2. book	7. book
3. took	8. hear
4. hear	9. carry
5. four	10. four

Write the Words in Sentences—II

1. state	6. grow
2. grow	7. river
3. river	8. state
4. once	9. Once
5. began	10. began

Choose the Correct Words

1. state	6. river
2. carry	7. grow
3. book	8. took
4. four	9. hear
5. began	10. once

Just-for-Fun Missing Letters

1. carry	6. began
2. state	7. once
3. took	8. hear
4. book	9. grow
5. river	10. four

Unit 28: ANSWER KEY

Find the Words—Level A

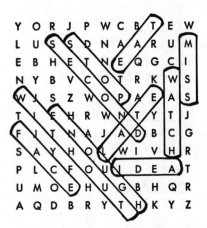

```
C M S E C O N D F H
R E N O U G H E A T
Z D A P O S T O P C
M I S S P U Q U G F
G O Q Y U S U C E A
B X A A T P A J S Y
J D A P L K R Z F P
N V W I T H O U T O
L A T E D W A T C H
O I D E A F A C E O
```

Find the Words—Level B

```
Y O R J P W C B T E W
L U S S D N A A R U M
E B H E T N E G G C I
N Y B V C O T R K W S
W J S Z W O P A E A S
T E H R W N T Y T J
F T N A J A D B C G
S A Y H O L W I V H R
P L C F O U N D E A T
U M O E H U G B H Q R
A Q D B R Y T H K Y Z
```

Write the Words in Sentences—I

1. eat	6. eat
2. miss	7. late
3. watch	8. miss
4. watch	9. late
5. enough	10. enough

Write the Words in Sentences—II

1. stop	6. stop
2. face	7. face
3. idea	8. second
4. without	9. without
5. second	10. idea

Choose the Correct Words

1. watch	6. enough
2. stop	7. idea
3. second	8. late
4. face	9. miss
5. eat	10. without

Just-for-Fun Anagrams

Answers will vary.

Unit 29: ANSWER KEY

Find the Words—Level A

```
Q D L Z I Z V Y H J M K
G X B P M A B O V E M M
H I N D I A N F A R Z L
A G L E T U X R L Y E P
M C T H M Y H U N Q O H
P O K P Y H D N N S V A
H U R E A L M O S T C A
R U T H C U T Q V U Y E
M R V B Y X L A C F Q J
S L I E K G R M A R H R
T K G S O M E T I M E S
G I R L M O U N T A I N
```

Find the Words—Level B

```
K Z A P M B C Y Q B Z C A
R W P L B A G I R L F Y H
X Q M H M T J V T Z B J
X V N X Y O E H U I G W B
K D J K S M S C D H T Y C
J U R C O O L T M C J O U
M B E K M U E D W C E U C
X S A C E N T J Z U J N I
U W L C T T Z L O N B F Z
W J L N I A Z O D R H F T
C C L U M I O I N D I A N
X B P G E N J H A B O V E
H M O L S F A R M N H P G
```

Write the Words in Sentences—I

1. Indian	6. girl
2. let	7. above
3. above	8. cut
4. cut	9. girl
5. Indian	10. let

Write the Words in Sentences—II

1. Sometimes	6. almost
2. mountain	7. Sometimes
3. far	8. far
4. real	9. almost
5. mountain	10. real

Choose the Correct Words

1. almost	6. above
2. sometimes	7. Indian
3. girl	8. cut
4. far	9. real
5. mountain	10. let

Just-for-Fun Word Mazes

1. girl	6. Indian
2. real	7. above
3. almost	8. far
4. sometimes	9. mountain
5. cut	10. let

Unit 30: ANSWER KEY

Find the Words—Level A

```
B O D Y  S O N G H
O M U S I C M E N
A Z Y F O G Y F W
O A H J K K T V W
A C O L O R Y H G
U T W F A M I L Y
M O Y O U N G W Q
T A L K S O O N P
L E A V E L I S T
```

Find the Words—Level B

Write the Words in Sentences—I

1. family	6. leave
2. song	7. color
3. color	8. music
4. music	9. leave
5. family	10. song

Write the Words in Sentences—II

1. talk	6. soon
2. body	7. young
3. young	8. talk
4. body	9. soon
5. list	10. list

Choose the Correct Words

1. body	6. soon
2. song	7. list
3. young	8. family
4. talk	9. color
5. music	10. leave

Just-for-Fun Letter Squares

1. talk	6. body
2. song	7. soon
3. leave	8. list
4. music	9. family
5. young	10. color